OWN YOUR MONEY

Quarto.com

© 2023 Quarto Publishing Group USA Inc.
Text © 2023 Michela Allocca

First Published in 2023 by Fair Winds Press, an imprint of The Quarto Group,
100 Cummings Center, Suite 265-D, Beverly, MA 01915, USA.
T (978) 282-9590 F (978) 283-2742

Fair Winds Press titles are also available at discount for retail, wholesale, promotional, and bulk purchase.
For details, contact the Special Sales Manager by email at specialsales@quarto.com or by mail at The Quarto Group,
Attn: Special Sales Manager, 100 Cummings Center, Suite 265-D, Beverly, MA 01915, USA.

27 26 25 24 23   1 2 3 4 5

ISBN: 978-0-7603-8112-0

Digital edition published in 2023
eISBN: 978-0-7603-8113-7

Names: Allocca, Michela, author.
Title: Own your money : Practical Strategies to Budget Better, Earn More, and
  Reach Your 6-Figure Savings Goals / Michela Allocca.
Identifiers: LCCN 2022056701 | ISBN 9780760381120 (trade paperback) |
  ISBN 9780760381137 (ebook)
Subjects: LCSH: Finance, Personal.
Classification: LCC HG179 .A55 2023 | DDC 332.024--dc23/eng/20221219
LC record available at https://lccn.loc.gov/2022056701

Illustration: Mara Penny

Printed in China

MICHELA ALLOCCA

OWN YOUR MONEY

Practical Strategies to Budget Better,
Earn More, and Reach Your
6-Figure Savings Goals

FAIR WINDS

Contents

Introduction

There is immense pressure on young adults to figure out their lives early on: You're told you need to get your dream job right out of college and start climbing the corporate ladder. Beyond the stress of establishing a lifelong career at such a young age, you may feel pressure to do things like move to a big city, have a cool apartment, maintain a bustling social life—the list goes on! It's hard. It's scary. And there's no blueprint for what to do . . . until now!

The Hardest Years of My Life Were the Best Thing That Happened to Me

You may know me as the creator behind Break Your Budget, but the journey that led to this book started years before I had my own platform. If I could rewind to the evening before I started my first job out of school as a business analyst, I would tell myself to buckle the hell up because things are about to get rocky for a very long time. That's because my first day of work was the commencement of what I call the "endless cycle:" Wake up. Run. Shower. Commute. Work. Commute. Repeat.

Okay, yes, there was good with the bad. I'm not going to lie; commuting into Boston wearing my suit and walking through huge, shiny doors in the heart of the Back Bay made me feel important. I grew up watching movies that glamorized working in the city, wearing professional outfits, making lots of money, and sitting in a high-rise office with panoramic views. Here I was, on my first day of work, living what felt like a movie! Also, I wanted this job. I worked my ass off to get a job at a Fortune 500 company in a competitive rotational program. I went through hours and hours of interview "Superdays"—which are marathon interview days—and case studies to get there.

Yet after the first week of living the corporate life, the only thing getting me through each day was knowing that my paycheck was on the way. I got paid every other Friday, and having a salary meant this was the most money I'd ever made. I couldn't wait to see what my bi-weekly check would be.

Friday rolled around, and the first thing I did when I woke up at 5:30 that morning was log into my bank account. My heart sank when I saw it. I was barely breaking $1,600, which was almost $300 less than what I thought it would be. Unfortunately, I didn't realize just how much tax would be taken out, and after the taxes were combined with the 5 percent that I was contributing to my 401(k), I felt defeated.

Over the course of the first few months in that job, I lived at home and saved as much money as I possibly could. I didn't have any system in place; I just tried to keep my spending to less than $500 a month so I could save around $2,500 each month. I knew if I wanted to move out of my parents' house (and live that part of the "dream"), I'd have to map out my expenses to make sure I could afford it. Average rent prices in Boston were more than $1,000 per month, which was nearly an entire paycheck for me. At the end of that first summer, I found a tiny apartment in the North End neighborhood of Boston. My portion of the rent was $900 for a tiny room. (It had one window and no closet.) All I could fit inside my room were a full-size bed with no frame and a dresser that fit only half of my clothes. But I figured rent was going to be my biggest expense, so if I could keep that low, I could have better control over my monthly spend.

That was the way my brain worked. I don't know how or why I thought about money this way. I obsessed over spending the least amount possible and getting the most out of every dollar. Over time, this had a detrimental effect on my mental health.

Once I moved and started having real bills and obligations, I knew it was time for me to put together a budget. At this point, I didn't have any financial goals or a plan in place. I just knew that keeping track of my spending was probably a good idea so that I could make sure I was saving. I started by tracking my expenses on the Notes app on my iPhone.

Every time I spent money, I wrote down the date, the amount, and what it was for. I had a separate note for each month, and I'd start by first writing down the expenses I knew I had to pay—such as rent and my train pass. I managed to do this for about two months, but it was hard to keep up with and I never actually tallied up my total. I also found that when I spent money and felt guilty about it, I just didn't write it down. And if I didn't write it down, it didn't happen, right? Right.

Ultimately, I decided to graduate to a spreadsheet in the hopes it would be a bit easier to visualize what was going on. I am a visual person, so laying out my expenses enabled me to actually see where my money was going. One day at work when I was bored, I opened up Excel and put together a very basic budget template. I had five overarching categories, and within each category I made a few subcategories. It looked a little like this:

Living Expenses

Rent	$900
Electricity	$90
Gas	$25
Internet	$35
Train pass	$80

Food

Groceries	$200
Restaurants	$300
Coffee	$50

Social

Going out/Ubers	$300
Alcohol	$40
Shopping	$100

Miscellaneous

Drugstore	$50
Gym	$115
Personal care	$75

Total Spending	$2,360
Total Savings	Whatever was left!

After a few months of tracking my spending and diligently saving, I learned how to get smart and optimize my budget. I could shift money out of categories in which I wasn't spending as much as I thought, and if I just didn't spend any money, I could save more and more. It started to become addictive to see my bank account grow. Mind you, all of my savings were in my checking account. I wasn't investing beyond my 401(k), and I hadn't opened any other accounts yet. I was just hoarding cash, which isn't the most strategic way to save, but at the time I didn't know any better.

I kept up this routine for about two years until I switched jobs. Long story short, I hated my first job. It took me months to find a new job that I was excited about, and once I finally did, there was a catch: I had to take a pay cut. Accepting this job was a turning point for me. I knew that if I were taking home less money, I'd need to continue being diligent with my spending and saving—even more than I had been before. Beyond that, I wanted to find ways to start making more money because I knew it would be a while before my salary changed.

This is when my business, Break Your Budget, was born. I had successfully saved and invested nearly $50,000 in just over two years by contributing to my 401(k), intentionally saving $1,000 per month by cutting my expenses mercilessly, and putting 100 percent of any bonus I received directly into savings. I now had friends and peers coming to me for tips and advice on how they could build a budget for themselves. Why couldn't I share that with more people?

Eventually, I started offering 1:1 budgeting consults to some of my followers. They would pay me in exchange for help building their budget. I couldn't believe it. Any extra money I made from doing this went directly into my savings. It was fun! I was side-hustling before side hustles were cool. It gave me something to look forward to after work and to pour my own creativity into.

Fast-forward a few months, and the world stopped as a global pandemic hit. You know the story . . . like so many others, I got sent home and had extra free time after work. So to keep busy, I took what I learned from my job and poured myself into Break Your Budget. I also took some online courses that taught me about branding, social media, website design, copywriting, and more. Basically, I sought out all the skills that I couldn't learn at my day job.

I turned into a machine. I would spend eight hours a day working my 9 to 5 job, and at 5 pm I'd pivot toward Break Your Budget, for which I'd spend three to four hours in the evenings talking to my 1:1 budget clients, creating content for my social media, starting an email newsletter, and building a website. I didn't know it then, but I was planting the seeds to something bigger than myself. It was fun, and it made me feel less alone during a very isolating time.

I built a comprehensive budgeting template to help manage my own finances, and eventually I started selling it to my followers. I was making videos on TikTok and answering DMs and questions on Instagram. Eventually, brands started reaching out to me to partner with them and start advertising their products on my page. As I took Break Your Budget more seriously, I realized how much potential it had to become my full-time gig. In August 2021, I packed my bags and moved out of my parents' house and across the country to California.

I quit my job after about six months in Los Angeles and haven't looked back since. I spent nearly five years working in corporate America, and it taught me a lot about myself, personal finances, life, and more.

I'm going to unpack every lesson from my own journey throughout this book, while also providing you with tactical tips that you can implement to avoid making the same mistakes that I did. Basically, I want you to accelerate your financial success and hit your goals as early as possible—but to enjoy the process as well.

Before we get into Chapter 1, I want to highlight a few of the most important lessons I've learned over the years:

LESSON #1
ONCE THE BILLS START, THEY NEVER STOP

Yes, on social media it looks like everyone around you is moving into a high-rise in a big city and having their moment. However, if you can move home after college for a period of time, I highly recommend it.

That's because once you move out after you graduate college and start paying bills, they literally. Never. Stop. You will always have rent or a mortgage to pay, along with all the other bills that come along with a place of your own. If I could do it over, I would have stayed home much longer and dealt with my daily commute. It would have allowed me to build up a more sizable nest egg, and it would have taken the financial pressure off me for those first few years out of college.

Culturally, the United States sets an expectation for people to become self-sufficient and independent very early on in life. In many other countries around the world, it's much more normal for young adults to move home after they go to university and stay there until they get married. This gives them ample time to work and save before entering the next phase of their lives. I hope in the future we in the U.S. normalize living at home.

NOTE: *It's important to recognize that moving home after college is a privilege. If you are in a situation where moving home isn't an option, consider living with roommates so you can split some of your bills and keep living costs down.*

IF YOU'RE SERIOUS ABOUT SAVING, YOU MUST PRIORITIZE AND MAKE SACRIFICES

When I decided to move to Boston, I sacrificed many of the comforts I had at home. I lived in a glorified closet, I had to do my laundry at a laundromat, and I walked everywhere to avoid paying for unnecessary rideshares or transportation. I did all these things to free up additional space in my budget to allocate to my savings.

Often, people who are not serious about making a difference in their finances will look for every excuse for why they can't save. Some of these are the same people who don't track their expenses, live alone in luxury apartments, and pay $300 a month to park their car in a city with public transport.

If your income is limited, you need to make sacrifices. Figure out what is and isn't important to you, and then adjust from there. You'll learn how to do this throughout the rest of this book, but using myself as an example, I decided to live with roommates in apartments that were less-than-ideal because I spent the majority of my time at work and out of the house. If your situation is different—let's say you work a remote job and spend a lot of time at home—you may choose to prioritize a nicer apartment and cut back on your social expenses or non-essential lifestyle expenses.

YOUR LIFE IS A RESULT OF YOUR CHOICES

If you take nothing else away from this entire book except for this lesson, then I consider it a success: Your life as an adult is the result of *your* choices. This is a tough pill to swallow, and many young adults struggle with this because for the majority of their lives, choices were made for them.

I want to make a disclaimer here. I understand that the playing field isn't equal for everyone, and some people are given an unfair advantage while others are left in the dust to figure things out on their own. That being said, there comes a point in time where you get to decide your life and your parents, guardian, or family are no longer deciding for you. Owning the responsibility you have for choices that you can make is important. The sooner you realize this and accept it, the better off you'll be. Don't waste time blaming other people for things in your life that go wrong; start making choices that benefit you long term.

YOU CAN FIND HAPPINESS WORKING A 9 to 5 JOB

Throughout this book, I often paint corporate America in a less-than-flattering light. That said, while the majority of my time working a 9 to 5 was a negative experience, many positives came from it. I had built-in development and learning opportunities, I was given access to tons of software and systems that enabled me to build my own business in my free time, I made a lot of friends whom I am still close with years later, I had a stable paycheck, I had the ability to close my laptop and turn off work at the end of the day, and I had benefits such as a 401(k) and health insurance.

You *can* find happiness working a corporate job. You just need to figure out what you like to do and how to operate in the workplace, and unfortunately to do that you also need to learn what you *don't* like to do. This part is tough, but it will take you down the path you need to be on.

I'm excited to start this journey with you. The chapters that follow provide a clean slate and clear strategies for how to move from lost and confused to confident and intentional with your money. The only requirements are a positive attitude and honesty with yourself. Are you ready?

Chapter One

Get Organized, Get Started

I've found the secret to getting ahead is just to get started. My starting salary when I graduated college felt like more money than I could even imagine. I thought I could move to Boston and live in a nice apartment and that I would be all set. Ha! When I look back, I realize how naive I was.

What I *didn't* know was that, in reality, thanks to taxes and my 401(k), I was taking home about $1,000 *less* per paycheck than I was actually getting paid. And I didn't realize this until that first direct deposit hit and I looked at my pay stub. "Okay," I thought, "I can figure out how to make this work."

So I lived in my parents' home for about three months, saved as much as possible, and then found an apartment and a roommate in the city—you've heard the story. It was at this moment that I realized the bills had officially started. And as I've mentioned before, once they start, they never turn off.

Spending money began to give me anxiety. All I could focus on was spending *as little as possible*; it didn't matter if it was inconvenient or impractical. I didn't have a plan in place, nor did I have any idea how much money I had beyond what was in my checking account.

I heard my coworkers and friends talk about opening different accounts, such as high-yield savings accounts (HYSA) and Roth IRAs (Individual Retirement Account). I didn't know what they were. They sounded like scams. And I was too scared to ask questions, so I just kept hoarding my money in my checking account, telling myself "I'll figure it out later." But when was "later?" I didn't know.

It took me years to learn how to optimize my money—to get a basic understanding of my situation beyond just my bi-weekly paycheck, how to get financially organized, how to find and set up the right accounts, and how to calculate my net worth. I could have taken enormous strides if I hadn't wasted so much time focusing on simply not spending any of my money. I now realize that the sooner you can take control of your finances and put together a plan, the sooner you will find success.

Pull the Blinds Back: What is Your Financial Situation Right Now?

Do you remember the bestselling book called *The Life-Changing Magic of Tidying Up* by Marie Kondo? It details how to declutter and organize every aspect of your life. The lesson is that if you take the time to do it just once, you'll never have to do it again.

When I read the book, I knew many of the lessons could apply to less tangible areas of my life, specifically my finances. Although tidying my finances wasn't something I could necessarily see in my day-to-day life in the same way I could see tidying my closet, it gave me a similar feeling. I felt organized, and as a result I made better financial decisions. I became more present and intentional with my approach to my money and finances. Thus, I decided to adopt the idea of minimalism to streamline my financial life.

To do this, I needed to dive deep on my finances. This can be intimidating, especially if you're starting from scratch or are unhappy with where you are at the moment. That being said, a full financial review is a crucial step in determining your financial direction. Here's why.

1. **IT PROVIDES A STARTING POINT:** How can you determine the direction you need to move in if you have no idea where you're starting? A financial review puts everything on the table, from your income and expenses to your assets and liabilities (which we'll get to later in this chapter).

2. **YOU CAN IDENTIFY BLIND SPOTS:** If you haven't taken inventory of your finances recently, it's likely you have some blind spots or problem areas that need to be addressed. For example, maybe there's a credit card you have forgotten about or an old checking account that you never closed.

3. **IT FORCES YOU TO GET ORGANIZED:** To take full inventory of your financial life, you have to organize your accounts and list out where all your money and debts are living. This process can actually relieve a lot of stress and provide direction on areas of consolidation, unused accounts, and more.

4. **YOU CAN SET CLEAR GOALS:** Starting on page 50, you will learn how to set financial goals correctly. However, it will be difficult to set a financial goal if you have no idea what you're working with. Taking inventory provides clarity so you can determine what you want to accomplish and when.

NOTE: *As you work through this chapter, I encourage you to get vulnerable. Allow yourself to feel the emotions that come up—whether it's judgment, fear, or guilt—and accept the situation for what it is, knowing that you are taking the steps to make things better.*

Your Financial Snapshot

Keeping our decluttering theme in mind, it's time to break down your finances and work through a full financial review. This involves way more than simply knowing your salary or monthly expenses. Your financial life is comprehensive, so it's important to understand both *what* you are working with and *why* your situation is what it is.

In this four-phase process, you will not only lay out every aspect of your financial situation, but you'll walk away with an understanding of *your why*. This is a methodical system—I will clarify the goal and the exact steps you need to take to complete each phase. By the end, you will have established an intimate relationship with your finances!

PHASE 1: LAYING THE GROUNDWORK

The first step is the hard part; it's working through every corner of your finances with a fine-tooth comb. You will want to grab a notebook and a pen, or pull up your favorite budgeting spreadsheet, to keep track of each account. By the end of this exercise, your goal is to have a personal database of every single account you have, from credit cards to investment accounts. It's time to make a list!

BANK ACCOUNTS: Create a list of every single bank account you have. This includes cash-flow accounts such as a checking account and savings accounts such as a high-yield savings account. For each, include the amount of money currently in the account as well as the purpose of the account. Is there anywhere you can consolidate?

DEBT ACCOUNTS: Identify every loan or debt that you currently owe. These could include, but are not limited to, student loans (federal or private), personal loans, car loans, and credit card debt. Be sure to include the loan service provider, the total loan amount, the total amount you currently owe, and the interest rate for each. This category can be hard to consolidate, but knowing how many loans you have can make future decisions about taking on more debt easier.

INVESTMENT ACCOUNTS: List any investment accounts you have opened, including all retirement accounts such as a 401(k) or an IRA and taxable brokerage accounts. Investment accounts also include any accounts you've opened with an investing app as well as crypto accounts. With each account, include the current balance as well as how frequently you contribute to it. This category is easy to clutter, especially if you change jobs and don't roll over your 401(k), so as you work through this, look for duplicate accounts.

CREDIT CARDS: Create a list of any credit cards you have open, including those you don't frequently use. For each card, be sure to identify the rewards that the card offers (cashback, travel, etc.) and the types of transactions you use it for. It is very easy to end up with multiple credit cards that become hard to keep track of. Having too many open cards can lead to racking up credit card debt, forgetting to pay off balances, accruing interest and, ultimately, a host of financial issues. Keep in mind, if you have a credit card under your parents' name, this will also impact your credit score, so include it as part of this list.

ARE CREDIT CARDS BAD?

Credit cards can be an amazing tool to help you build wealth. Yes, you read that right. When used correctly, credit cards can both aid in building strong credit and can help you score cashback or major travel deals.

Most credit cards offer rewards, whether it's money back on every purchase, money back on specific categories of purchases, or points that you can cash in for travel. The rate at which you earn points depends on the card you have or the purchase you make; for example, some travel cards will offer five times the amount of usual points on travel-related expenses, while a cashback card may offer 5 percent cashback on gas and 2 percent back on restaurants.

The best way to maximize the benefits of credit card rewards is to choose a card that aligns with your values and priorities. If you rarely travel, it's a better idea to go with a cashback card. If you love taking luxurious vacations, finding a travel card with lots of perks will give you more bang for your buck.

These days there are thousands of credit cards to choose from. My favorite resource for browsing different options with thorough breakdowns of fees, rates, rewards, pros, and cons is www.ThePointsGuy.com. He breaks down various card types, issuers, and rewards programs so it's easier to find the right credit card for your situation!

PHASE 2: ASSESS YOUR CASH FLOW

Now that you have combed through all of your accounts, it's time to review your cash flow. This is how you will understand when you have money flowing in and when that money ultimately flows out. Your goal in this section is to clearly define your income, your payment frequency, and the timing of recurring bills.

YOUR INCOME: Look at your income. How much do you make annually? What is your monthly take-home pay after tax and deductions? Having an intimate understanding of how much money you bring in is essential when planning expenses and setting financial goals.

PAYDAY FREQUENCY: How often do you get paid? When you get paid, where does the money go? Knowing the timing of your cash flow will help ensure that your bills get paid on time, that you don't overdraft any accounts, and that you can move money into savings, into investments, or toward debt payoff in an efficient manner.

DEDUCTIONS: Are there any deductions that come out of your paycheck before it clears your account? Some common examples—aside from tax—include 401(k) contributions, health insurance, HSA (health savings account) or FSA (flexible spending account) contributions, and other job-related and job-specific deductions. If you have any deductions, list them out and how much each is.

RECURRING BILLS: These include any bills that require an on-time payment. Some examples would be rent, utilities, insurance, and minimum debt payments. All of these are time-sensitive and require prompt payment to continue operation. List out when the payments are due, too.

PHASE 3: YOUR MONTHLY OUTPUT

With your cash flow in mind, it's time to turn to your monthly expenses. Knowing how much is coming in is meaningless without knowing how much is going *out*. After surveying your monthly expenses to determine your total monthly output by category, you should clearly understand your essential and non-essential expenses.

ESSENTIALS: Essential expenses include anything you need to pay to exist. They include your recurring bills—such as a mortgage payment or rent, utilities, and insurance—as well as transportation, groceries, and minimum debt payments. For each category, list out how much you spend on average each month and then add up your total. These are your total *baseline* expenses.

CREDIT SCORE

Building a strong credit score can pay dividends on your finances long term. It can help you secure lower rates on loans such as a mortgage or car note, get approved for higher credit limits, and look good to employers—the list goes on. But how is your credit score determined, and what's a good score?

There are five main factors that impact your credit score:

Payment history: Whether you pay your bills on time is the single biggest factor that determines your credit score.

Utilization: This is how much of your available credit you use on an average basis.

Age: This means not how old you are, but how long you've had your accounts open.

Mix: This means how many types of credit you have, including various credit cards, student loans, personal loans, car loans, etc.

Inquiries: Every time you apply for new credit, an inquiry is reported on your credit score.

Depending on the credit model, your score can range from 300 to 850. Any score that is more than 750 is considered excellent, while any score below 500 is considered poor.

NON-ESSENTIALS: These are any type of expense that you can live without, such as clothing, shopping, restaurants or dining out, entertainment, travel, gym memberships, and subscriptions, to name a few. For each non-essential category, list your average monthly spending. Then add up the averages.

PHASE 4: THE DETAILS

The final phase of taking your financial snapshot is assessing your situation's smaller details. This includes your credit score, any insurance policies you may own, and any inheritances you could be entitled to (if applicable). List out any additional financial information related to your credit score, insurance policies, or inheritances to complete your financial picture. Every detail counts.

CREDIT SCORE: If you have ever paid back debt—such as a student loan—or if you have a credit card, then you have a credit score. Your credit score is like your adult GPA; it is a numerical value that quantifies your credibility when it comes to paying back debt to banks or loan service providers. You can find your credit score on your bank or loan statement, or you can get it from a free credit score provider such as Credit Karma.

INSURANCE POLICIES: Insurance policies can be difficult to track. But it's likely you have health insurance, and if you have a car, you must have car insurance. Other common types of insurance include home, renters', life, disability, and long-term care insurance. Assess your situation: What types of insurance do you have, and how much do you pay for each?

INHERITANCES: If you have a trust or inheritance that you are aware of, spend time discussing the parameters of the accounts with a trusted family member. Although there may be guidelines or rules in place to determine when you gain access to the funds, it's important to have an idea of what to expect and when, should this apply to you.

This deep-dive process can take anywhere from thirty minutes to a couple of hours, depending on how many accounts you have and how organized you are from the start. Keeping all of this information in one central repository will make your entire financial process much easier and it can serve as a point of reference in the future. Every aspect of your finances matters. Now you should have a full picture of what you are working with.

Financial Framework for Success

No matter what your financial goals are, you need the proper accounts to reach them. Moving from the accounts you have to a more organized framework will give you an intentional foundation for your savings and investment goals over the course of your life. Here is what I recommend.

CASH FLOW ACCOUNT: You'll need a simple checking account to use as a repository for income. It should also be the account that your money flows out of for bills and other financial goals. You only need one.

INCONVENIENT SAVINGS: This is a high-yield savings account for short-term savings goals. You can have more than one, especially if you have multiple savings goals and like to keep them separate. If you have more than one account, make sure you name each one for its respective goal. I recommend choosing one bank for your high-yield savings accounts so you can access them in a single place.

RETIREMENT: There are many different retirement account options, such as a 401(k), 403(b), and IRA, to name a few. Identify 1 or 2 retirement accounts that are necessary for you; for most, this includes either a 401(k) or 403(b) and either a Roth or Traditional IRA.

TAXABLE INVESTING: Taxable investment accounts are for investing beyond retirement. They include a brokerage account, a crypto wallet, real estate, and more. The limits are endless, and as a result, taxable investing can easily become a category in which you have multiple accounts. Start with a brokerage account, and as your financial goals evolve, it's likely you will continuously add taxable accounts to your framework.

> NOTE: *The term* inconvenient *means that the money is separated from your usual cash flow and requires intentional thought to transfer money into savings and out of it. Inconvenient savings are dollars that are readily accessible but separate enough that it is inconvenient to withdraw the funds, so you are less likely to do so unless it is for the goal or entirely necessary. A great place for inconvenient savings is in an HYSA (see page 21).*

CASH FLOW
ACCOUNT

INCONVENIENT
SAVINGS

RETIREMENT

TAXABLE
INVESTING

Net Worth: The Most Important Measure of Your Finances

Now that you have spent time auditing every corner of your finances and put together your account framework, you have all of the information you need to calculate your net worth. To me, net worth is the most important measure of financial progress. It allows you to examine your finances holistically, beyond just your income or expenses. If your net worth is growing, that indicates you are accumulating wealth, which is the ultimate goal of any financial journey.

WHAT IS NET WORTH?

Net worth is your total wealth as an individual, taking into account all your assets and liabilities. In simple terms, it's the amount of money you'd have if you were to sell everything you had (including any investments) and pay off all your debts.

The goal is to have a positive net worth that is continuously growing. As you increase your savings rate and invest more money while simultaneously paying off your debt, your net worth grows. This is because your assets are increasing while your debts are decreasing.

ASSETS – LIABILITIES = NET WORTH

NET WORTH EQUATION

To calculate your net worth, subtract your total liabilities from your total assets. To do this, you'll need to tally up all of your savings and investments, as well as the total debt that you currently owe. With this information, you can do some quick math and determine your current net worth.

Keep in mind that your net worth is ever-changing. If it's currently negative, don't freak out! It's very common to have a negative net worth, especially if you are young, have just graduated college and have student loans, or haven't taken the time to examine your finances before now. The purpose of this calculation is to provide a starting point for building wealth over the course of your life.

As you progress through your financial journey, you will be paying off debt, saving, and investing; thus, your net worth will increase over time. Knowing your net worth allows you to measure your progress, so keeping track of its growth on a consistent basis is key.

WAYS TO INCREASE YOUR NET WORTH

Increasing your net worth has obvious benefits. Aside from serving as an indicator of financial health, a positive and growing net worth can help you feel financially secure and even allow you to retire years earlier.

Here are a few ways you can start increasing your net worth. Remember that you don't need to do all of these at once!

PAY DOWN YOUR DEBT: Debt can be a drag, especially high-interest credit card debt. Prioritizing debt repayment is a surefire way to steadily increase your net worth. Luckily, you've already assessed your debt situation, so you're equipped with the information you need to put together a debt payoff strategy.

BOOST RETIREMENT CONTRIBUTIONS: If you utilize tax-advantaged accounts to save for retirement, you can reduce your tax bill while investing your money to grow long term. Taking advantage of a tax-efficient strategy over the course of your working life will help you save more money and boost your net worth.

INCREASE YOUR INCOME: An obvious way to save and invest more money is to make more money. With more money coming in, you can pay down your debt faster and invest more, amplifying your net-worth growth. You can do this by advocating for a promotion or a raise at work, starting a side hustle, or picking up a part-time job (see Chapter 8).

THE BOTTOM LINE

Increasing your net worth is a marathon, not a sprint. It takes time to see financial growth, and it can be difficult to prioritize multiple financial goals at once. Over the next few chapters, I am going to guide you through the process of creating your own financial strategy by building a budget, setting goals, learning how to spend, and more.

Your net worth will be growing before you know it!

DEBT PAYOFF STRATEGIES

Paying off debt is no easy feat. You can implement either of two strategies into your broader financial plan to accelerate paying off your debt: the Avalanche Method and/or the Snowball Method.

Debt Avalanche: The Avalanche Method focuses on prioritizing debt based on interest rate. When using this method, you would first make the minimum payments on your outstanding debt. Then you would focus on paying off the debt with the highest interest rate first. This is a very efficient method; by paying off the debt with the higher interest first, you reduce the total amount of interest you pay over the lifetime of the loan.

Debt Snowball: The Snowball Method focuses on prioritizing debt based on balance amount by loan. When using this method, you would first make the minimum payments on your outstanding debt. Then you would focus on paying off the debt with the smallest balance first to "get it out of the way." This helps build momentum as you progress toward paying off your debts with larger balances. This method is designed to increase motivation. As you pay off smaller loans in full, you gain momentum and it "snowballs" into more progress on the bigger loans. Because you see fast results by paying off the smaller loans first, you are more likely to stick to your debt payoff plan over time.

Both of these strategies assume you have additional money to put toward debt beyond your minimum payments. The type of debt you have can help determine which payoff strategy is a better fit for your situation. If you have a lot of high-interest credit card debt, it is a better idea to use the Avalanche Method. If you have student loans that have a lower interest rate, the Snowball Method may be more efficient.

CHAPTER 1 MONEY REVIEW

The secret to getting ahead with your finances is taking the first step: A full financial review has a ton of benefits, most notably providing a starting point, helping you to identify blind spots, aiding your financial organization, and clearing the path to set goals.

A financial snapshot puts you in the driver's seat of your financial life: This four-phase process will help you uncover your *why* behind improving your situation long-term. Working through this exercise will lay the foundation of your financial future. The four phases include auditing your bank accounts, assessing your cash flow, understanding your monthly output, and reviewing all of the extra details.

Following a framework will keep your finances minimal and organized: Having the proper accounts will enable you to reach your financial goals. I recommend a checking account, a high-yield savings account, a retirement account, and a taxable investing account.

Your net worth measures your financial health: I equate net worth to a financial pulse check. It allows you to examine your financial situation by taking away the more common measures we gravitate toward: your salary and expenses. A growing net worth indicates you are accumulating wealth—which is far more important than simply increasing your salary.

There are only two ways to increase your net worth: You can either save and invest more money or you can pay down debt. Doing both at the same time is an ideal combination and will accelerate your progress.

Credit scores are your adult GPA: Even though it is often overlooked, your credit score can dictate your financial future. A low credit score can make it difficult to qualify for a loan, while a high credit score can help you secure lower interest rates and save money over time.

CHAPTER 1 ACTION ITEMS

Work through a financial snapshot (1 hour): You can do this by using the worksheet available on page 164 or by purchasing The Personal Finance Dashboard, which is available at www.breakyourbudget.com. Take inventory of every account you have, making note of the purpose of the account and the balance in the account. Then, pull up your most recent paycheck and write down your gross income, net income, tax payments, and deductions. The last step is to list out your monthly recurring expenses—don't forget to include the day each expense occurs or is due, as well as the account or card you pay it from.

Open your new accounts (1 hour): If you need to open a high-yield savings account or IRA, enroll in your 401(k) or 403(b), or open a taxable investing account, do it now! You can identify the accounts you need by reviewing your financial snapshot and noting which accounts within the financial framework you have already and which you still need to open.

Calculate your net worth (10 minutes): This should be easy once you complete your financial snapshot. You can add up the account balances you have and then subtract your various debts, if you have them. The result of this quick math is your net worth. Write it down, along with the date you are calculating it. This can serve as your starting point on your financial journey!

Budget Is Not a Bad Word

....

Having a budget doesn't have to suck. Yes, budgeting has a bad reputation, but I believe this is because most people have the completely wrong idea about budgets. They associate them with restriction and cutting corners. They think, "If I follow a budget, I will have to eat rice and ramen for every meal," or "I'll have to pass on the appetizer every time I go out to dinner."

But the real purpose of having a budget is just the opposite! It's designed to help you avoid feeling like you need to cut corners in every aspect of your life. A budget that is built effectively should actually *feel* nothing like a budget at all—at least in the traditional sense.

A budget is another word for having a plan; it should feel like it, too. An effective budget assigns every dollar to a specific purpose that works toward one of three objectives: paying your bills, accomplishing your financial goals, and funding your passions. A budget that does this allows you to decide ahead of time what *you want to do* with your money, rather than your money deciding for you.

....

Budget Myth-busting

There are many common misconceptions about budgeting that hold people back from taking their first step toward financial success. But the truth is, many people use these misconceptions as an excuse to avoid doing what they know they need to do: build a budget. Let's smash a few of the major misconceptions, one by one.

Budget Myth	What You Mean	Myth-buster
Building and following a budget takes too long.	"I don't want to budget."	Creating your very first budget is going to take some time. However, if you put in some time and effort up front, maintaining a budget is actually very simple and can be done in as little as ten minutes or less on a weekly basis.
If I have a budget, I can't have any fun.	"Budgeting is too restrictive and I want to live my life."	Your budget can be what gives you permission to spend! When you have your monthly costs laid out, you can dedicate funds to whatever is most important to you.
Budgets are for poor people.	"I make enough money, so I don't need to pay attention to it in the same way other people do."	Making a lot of money and having a lot of money are two different things. It doesn't matter how much you make; it matters how much you keep. A person earning $50,000 but saving $10,000 annually is more successful than someone earning $100,000 but saving nothing.

At the end of the day, a budget is a tool you can use to handle your money. In the same way that you would create an exercise regimen to tone up for the summer or put together a plan before launching a business, you can create a budget to be your roadmap for getting from where you are right now to where you want to be in the future.

It doesn't need to be complicated or high-maintenance; it just needs to be *effective*. Even if you don't think you need one or don't feel ready yet, build it anyway. You'll be surprised what you can uncover through the process!

Building a Foolproof Budget

There are many different ways to build a budget. It's likely that every person you ask—from family and friends to financial gurus—will tell you something different. Here's my take: There are varying degrees and levels of detail to each and every budget. However, all budgets follow the same equation: income - expenses. You can take this equation as far as you'd like; the deeper you go, the more detail you'll extract, and the more effective your budget and financial decision-making will become.

STEP 1: ZERO-BASED BUDGETING

Every successful budget has two main elements: income and expenses. Simply put, to build a budget, you need to have an income and then subtract out all your expenses. There are three potential outcomes of this simple equation: a surplus, a shortfall, or zero.

With a *surplus*, you have more money left over at the end of the month than what you have spent. This means you have money to put toward something else (whether that is a financial goal or a purchase is up to you).

With a *shortfall*, you don't make enough money to cover your expenses. To put it bluntly, this means you either need to increase your income or you need to trim your expenses.

When your budget outcome is *zero*, this means you've successfully accounted for every dollar that you've earned. This is the definition of a zero-based budget.

SURPLUS   **ZERO**    **SHORTFALL**

Zero-based budgeting is one of the most effective ways to build out a budget for a few key reasons:

1. **YOU'VE GIVEN EVERY DOLLAR THAT YOU EARN A PURPOSE.** With this type of budget, every dollar has to be allocated *somewhere*, whether it's toward an expense or toward a goal. This means you need to be fully aware of how much money flows in and out and where it is going.

2. **YOU ARE INTENTIONAL.** Because every dollar has a purpose, you are forced to think about where and why you are dedicating money to certain obligations. If something isn't working, it needs to be shifted to get back to zero.

3. **YOUR GOALS BECOME A PRIORITY.** No more treating savings as whatever is "left over" at the end of the month. With a zero-based budget, savings are built in as an expense and must be allocated to balance the equation.

Now that you understand zero-based budgeting and its importance, you're ready to take it to the next level. You've got your income and expenses ready to go, but you want to take it a bit deeper so it becomes easier to allocate your income back to zero.

That is where the three-bucket budget comes into play.

STEP 2: THE THREE-BUCKET BUDGET

A three-bucket budget is exactly what it sounds like—a budget that is broken up into three buckets. These buckets are essentials, financial goals, and non-essentials, and you will need to consider them in that order.

ESSENTIALS

Your essentials are your necessary costs—in other words, your costs to simply exist. These are your recurring or monthly expenses that you *have to spend*. Generally speaking, essentials are difficult to reduce but they stay steady month over month. Although they may fluctuate slightly, you can anticipate what they will be on a consistent basis.

They include the following, at a minimum:

- Living expenses (rent or mortgage, utilities such as electricity and internet)
- Insurance (medical, home, auto, etc.)
- Prescriptions/medicine
- Groceries
- Transportation (car payment, gas, subway ticket)
- Minimum debt payments (These are considered essential expenses because they are *obligations you have previously agreed to*. You are obligated to pay these; they are not expenses you can trim or reduce. Any debt payments beyond the minimum payment would count as a financial goal, which I will get into shortly.)

NOTE: *List out all of your essentials and include both 1) what they are and 2) how much you spend on them each month (look back to Chapter 1, where you did this already). Add them up: This total is your monthly baseline, and it can serve as a shortcut for identifying how much you need to keep as emergency savings. A great way to figure out how much money should be in your emergency savings is to multiply your baseline by either three or six months, depending on whether you have a steady income (such as a corporate job) or a variable income (if you work hourly or for yourself).*

FINANCIAL GOALS

Your financial goals are the goals you are working toward in both the short term and the long term. I will dive deep on how to effectively and strategically set financial goals for yourself in the next chapter, but for now it's important to understand why they come directly after your essential expenses, and also what constitutes a financial goal.

SAVINGS

INVESTING

DEBT-PAYOFF

Financial goals are one of the main reasons why you need a budget in the first place. It's likely you wanted to begin budgeting in an effort to save more money, or maybe to pay off some debt. However, it's very common to forget this in the process of building a budget if you become hyper-focused on your expenses rather than your savings.

Financial goals need to be a priority, so when you are creating a zero-based, three-bucket budget, put them directly after essentials but *before* non-essentials. By doing this, you'll ensure that you don't treat financial goals as "whatever is leftover at the end of the month." They are part of the process and become part of the broader financial plan when they are factored into your monthly output.

Think of each financial goal as an expense; you subtract this figure from your income on your way to reaching zero. Financial goals deserve attention, and if you are serious about reaching them, make room for prioritizing them.

There are three types of financial goals: savings goals, investing goals, and debt payoff goals. Once you have defined what each of these are for you, it becomes easier to prioritize and build them into your broader budget.

SAVINGS GOALS: Emergency fund, vacation, car, any major purchase

INVESTING GOALS: Retirement, real estate, brokerage, crypto

DEBT PAYOFF: Student loans, credit card, car loan, mortgage

NON-ESSENTIAL EXPENSES

Your non-essential expenses are the last area of a three-bucket budget. These expenses are "everything else"—that's any money you spend that is not going directly toward an essential expense or a financial goal.

This is the money you use to fund your passions; it's your fun money. It's the money you spend on hobbies, nurturing relationships, travel, and the list goes on. What are the activities that fuel you?

In Chapter 3, we will dive deep into how to most effectively spend your discretionary money and allocate your non-essential budget. Once you've determined your baseline essential expenses and your financial goals, you can quickly determine how much money you have to put toward discretionary spending and what you'd like to spend it on.

With these three buckets of money, you can put together an extremely effective budget. But let's take it a step further!

STEP 3: 50/30/20 BUDGETING

If you love the idea of a three-bucket budget but aren't sure how much to allocate to certain areas, the 50/30/20 budget is your solution.

This budgeting method takes your three buckets—essentials, financial goals, and non-essentials—and provides a framework for how much of your income to allocate to each.

Here's the simple breakdown:

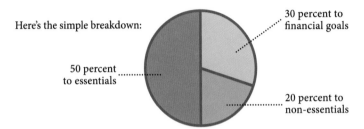

50 percent to essentials

30 percent to financial goals

20 percent to non-essentials

Traditional financial experts approach the 50/30/20 method slightly differently than I do, most commonly by switching financial goals and non-essentials in the hierarchy (30 percent to non-essentials and 20 percent to financial goals).

I don't like this for two main reasons:

1. If you're serious about your financial goals, they need to be a higher priority. Meaning, you need to dedicate more of your income to them than you do in other areas.

2. The difference in quality of life between 20 and 30 percent allocated to non-essentials isn't enough to de-prioritize your goals; but the difference in saving or investing that additional 10 percent can translate to hundreds of thousands of dollars in the future. Focus on value-based spending, which we will learn about in Chapter 4, and use your discretionary income very intentionally.

You can take your three-bucket budget and allocate your expenses to fit within the 50/30/20 framework. Remember, these parameters are designed to serve as a *guideline*. You can adjust them as necessary if you find they don't fit your current situation.

Budgeting Tools

Now that you have worked through methods for building out your budget, it's time to move on to another very important part of effective budgeting: the tool you use. There is a lot of debate in the personal finance universe around using a spreadsheet versus using a budgeting app, and here is my take.

It doesn't matter as long as you actually use it!

At the end of the day, the key purposes of a budgeting tool are tracking your expenses, visualizing how and where you spend your money, and gaining insight you can use to make smarter financial decisions.

An effective budgeting tool will have three main features:

1. **A PLACE TO BUILD A BUDGET.** You can map out your income and expenses by category, while also incorporating your financial goals.

2. **A PLACE TO TRACK YOUR EXPENSES.** This is where you actually input what you are spending money on and how much you spend.

3. **A PLACE THAT PROVIDES INSIGHTS.** Planning and tracking is great, but you need to use that information to make smarter decisions. The tool you choose should provide insights around how you're spending so you can make continuous improvements.

Do you prefer to manage your finances manually or let an app do the heavy lifting for you? Let's consider the pros and cons of both choices and what to look for when choosing your tool.

BUDGETING SPREADSHEETS

A simple budgeting spreadsheet is an excellent way to get started. This way you can customize the categories you choose to track and make your money management process as simple or as comprehensive as you'd like.

BENEFITS OF A SPREADSHEET

IT'S FULLY CUSTOMIZABLE. You can choose which categories you want to track and drill into your finances as far as you'd like to. If you're someone who loves detail, this is a dream. You can also create your own features, such as graphs or tables, which will cater to the insights *you* want to see and use for financial decision-making.

YOU BECOME MORE INTENTIONAL WITH YOUR FINANCES. To optimize a spreadsheet budget, you need to manually record everything you want to see. Therefore, you stay very close to your finances and there is virtually no way for expenses to fall off your radar. As a result, you have a heightened awareness of each and every expense. Knowing where your money is going, and taking the time to record each expense, will make you much more intentional about your spending decisions. Ultimately, this helps influence and change spending behavior over time, which will make you more comfortable with and confident about your spending choices.

IT CAN BECOME A SHARED TOOL. Life changes are inevitable. A spreadsheet can become a tool shared with a partner or even grow into a family planning tool. This flexibility makes it a great choice for longevity.

CONS OF A SPREADSHEET

IT IS MANUAL. You have to enter each expense or transaction you choose to track, so it is a more time-consuming option.

IT CAN BE HARD TO KEEP UP WITH. Because spreadsheets are manual, you only get out what you put in. This means if you go a couple of weeks without checking in on it, you may fall behind and struggle to catch up, which leads to losing motivation and ignoring your budget altogether.

THEY CAN BE COMPLEX AND INTIMIDATING. If you don't have a lot of knowledge or experience with spreadsheets and formulas, this type of tool can feel overwhelming. The tool you choose should be one that you feel comfortable with and confident about—and if you don't know how to actually create a spreadsheet, it may not be the right option.

IS A BUDGET SPREADSHEET RIGHT FOR YOU?

If you decide to use the spreadsheet option, you will need to commit around fifteen minutes per week or around one hour per month to updating it to get the most out of the tool. You will also need to familiarize yourself with spreadsheet maintenance and formulas, which can feel overwhelming if it's not something you've ever done before.

However, there are many benefits of using a spreadsheet. You can build an intimate relationship with your spending because you are forced to intentionally record each transaction. As a result, you'll be able to quickly change your financial behavior for the better and see improvements almost immediately.

If you are ready to make the commitment, a spreadsheet is an excellent option. It is also my personal preference, as I have used one to manage my finances for years. But if you're not ready to commit to a spreadsheet, there are plenty of other options!

BUDGETING APPS

Budgeting apps are the new and improved twenty-first-century tool for money management. The apps are designed for use on your smartphone and use artificial intelligence technology to monitor and track your spending automatically.

To start using a budgeting app, all you need to do is choose which one you'd like to download, sync up your bank accounts, and let the app do the rest of the heavy lifting for you. Budgeting apps will automatically track and categorize your expenses, and some will even provide suggestions on how you should build your budget based on how you've spent in the past. The apps have also become increasingly robust, with some now offering services to save automatically, negotiate your bills, or even identify and cancel subscriptions for you.

Sounds amazing, right?

BENEFITS OF BUDGETING APPS

THEY ARE AUTOMATIC. All you need to do is connect your bank accounts, and the budgeting apps do all the work for you. You may need to do some up-front setup, including choosing your categories and syncing all your accounts, but beyond that, the apps use technology to automatically track and categorize every transaction. You don't need to mess around with formulas, creating charts, or deciding what to track. This saves a lot of time, which is helpful if you're a busy person!

YOU GET REAL-TIME INFORMATION IN ONE PLACE. Many apps allow you to connect more than just your bank account; you can connect credit cards, retirement accounts, savings accounts, loans, and more. By connecting all this information in one central place, you can get real-time data at the tap of a button rather than needing to log into multiple sites to get the same information in a disjointed manner.

YOU CAN EASILY AVOID MAKING MISTAKES. Because the apps connect directly to your different accounts, you can ensure that every transaction or transfer is captured. If you don't check it for a few weeks, it is still working for you. Plus, many apps have an option for setting up automatic alerts, so they'll notify you if your bank balance is low, if there is an abnormal charge on your credit card, or if you're late on a payment.

CONS OF BUDGETING APPS

THEY'RE AUTOMATIC. Wait, didn't I just say this was a benefit? Well, it depends on how you look at it! Although automatic tracking saves a lot of time and effort, it adds a layer between you and your finances. This makes it much harder to become intentional with how you spend, because you aren't required to log every transaction. As a result, it becomes easier to ignore or overlook expenses, and it may take longer to see progress or change financial behavior.

CUSTOMIZATION IS LIMITED. Many apps have pre-determined categories and budgets that are pre-built. Oftentimes, you can't change the category names or remove those you don't want to see, which can make your budget feel clunky. It can be hard to build a budget you feel good about if you're unable to make it your own.

THEY OFTEN GET IT WRONG. Because apps are powered by artificial intelligence, they are simply looking for patterns to use to categorize your expenses and make recommendations. Because of this, they often miscategorize expenses and skew your information, which can be frustrating. Beyond that, they may make recommendations based on incorrect data, which can become overwhelming and annoying.

THEY COLLECT YOUR DATA. Budgeting apps are secure, meaning your personal banking information is not at risk. But the company behind the app can still collect all your data and sell it to third parties. If this is something that concerns you, keep it in mind when deciding what tool you'll use.

IS A BUDGETING APP RIGHT FOR YOU?

Budgeting apps make money management simple and accessible, as long as you have access to a smartphone. If you're a busy person, or if you're overwhelmed by spreadsheets and formulas, a budgeting app is an excellent option because it does a lot of the hard work for you, making the entire budgeting process really easy.

But if you aren't careful, it can be easy to overlook expenses and lose control of your budget while using an app. Plus, if you prefer a higher degree of customization, a budgeting app may not be the best choice for you.

At the end of the day, the best tool for you is *the tool you will actually use*. You can build a highly successful and effective budget with either a spreadsheet or an app, as long as you are consistent with checking in.

Keeping track of your money can be difficult, but it is a necessary step if you want to take control of your financial life. And the right tool can make budgeting easy . . . and maybe even fun!

	SPREADSHEETS	BUDGETING APPS
PROS	They are fully customizable	They are automatic
	You become more intentional with your finances	You get real-time information in one place
	They can become a shared tool	You can easily avoid making mistakes
CONS	They are manual	They are automatic
	They can be hard to keep up with	Customization is limited
	They can be complex and intimidating	They often get it wrong
		They collect your data

CHAPTER 2 MONEY REVIEW

Many people avoid making a budget by finding an excuse: Budgeting doesn't need to be complicated, boring, or restrictive. When you follow a methodical approach and weave in flexibility, you can create a budget that you'll finally be able to stick to!

The most efficient budget is zero-based: By allocating every dollar of income you earn to either an expense or a financial goal, you ensure that you aren't treating your savings as "leftovers." With a zero-based budget, every dollar has a purpose.

Your budget can be as detailed or as high-level as you want it to be: By following the three-bucket budget framework, you can go into as much or as little detail as you'd like so long as you divide your income into three buckets: essentials, financial goals, and non-essentials, in that order. You can take it a step further by allocating your income following the 50/30/20 framework.

The secret to success is a tool that you'll actually use: Choosing the right tool can make or break your budget. The key is to pick a tool you actually enjoy using, whether it's a spreadsheet, a budgeting app, or just a simple pen and paper. How do you want to approach your money, and which are you most likely to return to consistently?

CHAPTER 2 ACTION ITEMS

Identify your income: How frequently do you get paid, and what do you take home per paycheck and per month? Your income dictates the remainder of your budget, and it's important to figure out what you are working with *first*.

List out your essential expenses: These expenses will constitute your *baseline* budget. What expenses do you need to incur each month to survive? Write down what they are and how much they are, on average, each month.

List out your non-essential expenses: In chapter 4, you will learn how to more efficiently allocate these expenses and spend your money on things that add value to your life. In the meantime, list out what you are currently spending on non-essentials and how much, on average, each month. This will provide a starting point to work with when optimizing your budget.

List out any financial goals you are currently working toward: In a future chapter you will learn how to set SMART financial goals; but for now, list out any goals you are working toward at the moment and how much you are currently allocating to them each month.

Do some back-of-the-napkin math: Based on the numbers you just identified, subtract your expenses and goals from your income. Did you reach zero, or do you have a surplus or shortfall? Keep this information in mind throughout the rest of the book!

How to Set and Reach Your Financial Goals

The first financial goal I ever set for myself was to spend as little as possible. Little did I know that my goal would end up forging a toxic relationship with spending for many years to come. As I started to make money and get a consistent paycheck I could rely on, I found that saving money, and thus holding on to as much of my income as I could, became addictive. There was something satisfying about seeing a paycheck hit and that number in my checking account go up and up and up.

What became apparent over time was that as the figure continued to increase, my desire to spend began to decline. Because my only goal was to spend as little as possible, it got to a point that doing any type of activity that would cost money was unappealing to me. It took me more than a year to realize how toxic this mindset had become.

Once I set a few financial goals for myself, I learned that I could achieve them while also spending money—what a concept! It was a lapse in judgment for me that, looking back, feels really sad if I think about all of the activities and experiences I passed up in the name of saving money.

Financial goals provide direction; but beyond that, they create freedom. They allow you to decide *what* you want to accomplish, *when* you want to accomplish it, and *how* you plan to do so.

The first years out of college are some of the hardest for figuring out what exactly you want to do with your life, which is why setting financial goals during that time can be especially hard. Many young adults make the same mistake I did; they focus on spending as little as possible while simultaneously not taking the time to become financially literate. Others do the exact opposite; they ignore their money entirely until they realize they've dug themselves into a deep hole of debt that is hard to get out of.

It doesn't have to be this way. A small amount of forethought combined with an equal amount of planning can completely transform your twenties so that it's a time full of experience and fiscal responsibility.

Setting Financial Goals the Right Way

Take a moment to think about the last time you asked someone for directions. (Well, it's the twenty-first century, so if you haven't asked for directions recently, maybe think about the last time you used a maps app.) Chances are, you entered a starting point, which was where you were standing at that moment, and just as important, *an end point*, which is where you hoped to go.

Have you ever been able to get directions without an end point? Most likely, the answer to that question is *no*. How can you get directions to nowhere? You can't!

When it comes to planning your finances, you need to have an end point in mind; that end point is a financial goal. Financial goals give you a sense of *direction*; they help you define your path from where you currently are, which is your starting point, to where you want to be, which is your end point.

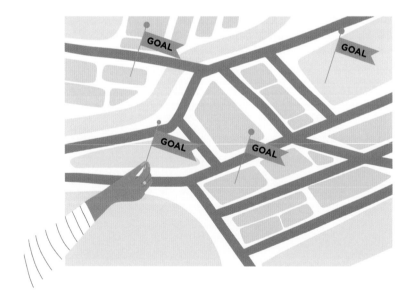

With a goal in mind, you can work backwards to figure out the necessary steps you need to take to reach it, and from there you can decide what is and is not feasible for you based on your situation.

It's really difficult to build a comprehensive financial plan without structured goals, and in this chapter we're going to learn how to set them the right way.

SMART Goal-Setting Method

Setting goals can feel intimidating. You may have a general idea of things you want to accomplish, which is *a desire*, but very few people take the next step toward achieving it.

The next step would be writing the goal down, which is when a desire becomes a verifiable *idea*. And for the overachievers (which is the category that all of you who are reading this book fall into), you have one more phase: creating a plan. Creating a plan transforms the idea into an *action*.

Now, in order to take a *desire* and transform it into an *action*, you have to follow a few different steps. It boils down to a tried-and-true goal-setting method: the SMART Method.

The SMART Method is used to guide the process of goal-setting. It's an acronym that stands for **S**pecific, **M**easurable, **A**chievable, **R**elevant, and **T**imely. Let me explain.

Specific: The goal is clear and well-defined. You have clarified exactly what you plan to accomplish.

Measurable: The goal has a quantifiable output; you have criteria that will define your progress toward accomplishing the goal.

Achievable: The goal is attainable and realistic for you to achieve.

Relevant: The goal is within reach and relevant to your life.

Timely: The goal has a defined deadline.

By using this method, you can focus your efforts on defining the steps you'll need to take to make your goal achievable and realistic, ultimately transforming it from a simple *desire* to a concrete *action*.

Now, let's break down each layer of the SMART Method a bit further.

SPECIFIC GOALS

When setting your specific goals, ask yourself the following questions:

- What needs to be accomplished for me to reach the goal?
- Who is responsible for it?
- What steps do I need to take?
- Why do I want to achieve this goal?

By laying out answers to these questions, you can dig into the deeper reasoning behind *why* you want to set this goal in the first place. This is an important step in creating motivation for accomplishing the goal.

Example: *I want to save a down payment for a house in Austin, Texas, by saving a portion of my paycheck every two weeks so that I can have a secure and reliable place to start a family with my partner.*

This goal is ultra-specific:

- What needs to be accomplished for me to reach the goal? *Save enough money for a down payment for a house.*
- Who is responsible for it? *I am responsible for the goal.*
- What steps do I need to take? *Set aside a portion of my paycheck every two weeks.*
- Why do I want to achieve this goal? *To have a secure and reliable place to start a family with my partner.*

MEASURABLE GOALS

Measurable goals provide criteria that you will use to determine your progress toward reaching your goal. You define that criteria during the goal-setting process by answering the following questions:

- How much do you need to save/invest/pay in total?
- How will you know when you have reached the goal?
- How frequently will you update your progress toward the goal?

Having a measurable, quantifiable goal is the first step in setting out your roadmap for actually achieving it. Let's elaborate on the example goal from earlier:

Example: *I want to save up **$20,000** for a down payment for a house in Austin, Texas, by saving **5 percent** of my paycheck every two weeks so that I can have a secure and reliable place to start a family with my partner. I will review this progress **once a month**.*

We've now put in measurable parameters that serve as success criteria for reaching this goal.

NOTE: *Following the SMART Method forces you to examine your goals from every angle. At the beginning of your financial journey, focusing on these details can help you identify your values and priorities, which makes it easier to understand what is and isn't important to you.*

ACHIEVABLE GOALS

This is where you bring yourself back to reality with your goal-setting process.

- Is what you are setting out to accomplish realistic?
- Do you have the resources or necessary capabilities to achieve it?

If a goal is totally unattainable, it's not efficient to focus time or energy on it. This is where you determine whether you have the resources and skill set necessary to reach it, or if you need to scale back your plans. A goal should be just challenging enough so it feels slightly out of reach, but it should also be thoroughly defined enough (through the first two steps) that you can actually make it happen.

Using our down-payment example, this person realized that reaching $20,000 by saving 5 percent of her income would take years. After some research, she learned she can still buy a home with a smaller down payment, so she adjusted her goal accordingly.

Example: *I want to save up **$10,000** for a down payment for a house in Austin, Texas, by saving **5 percent** of my paycheck every two weeks so that I can have a secure and reliable place to start a family with my partner. I will review this progress once a month.*

RELEVANT GOALS

This is where you take the goal and put it into perspective in your life. How does the goal fit into the big picture of your life direction? Is it relevant to the experiences and lifestyle you hope to live?

With our down-payment example, let's imagine this person has been renting an apartment for ten years. She is planning to get married within three years and start a family soon thereafter.

She updates her SMART goal to include this information:

Example: *I want to save up $10,000 for a down payment for a house in Austin, Texas, by saving 5 percent of my paycheck every two weeks so that I can have a secure and reliable place to start a family with my partner. I will review this progress once a month.* ***Since I no longer want to rent, and I plan to get married and start a family within the next three years, purchasing a home is the next step I need to take to achieve financial and emotional security.***

TIMELY GOALS

Timely goals include a deadline—this means you need to clearly define *when* you plan to achieve this goal. Having a deadline, combined with *measurable* criteria, will help break down the goal into digestible increments that you can then factor into your broader plan.

Wrapping up our down-payment example, let's add a timely deadline.

Example: *I want to save up $10,000 for a down payment for a house in Austin, Texas, by saving 5 percent of my paycheck every two weeks so that I can have a secure and reliable place to start a family with my partner. I will review this progress once a month. Since I no longer want to rent, and I plan to get married and start a family within the next three years, purchasing a home is the next step I need to take to achieve financial and emotional security.* ***I will achieve this savings goal in three years.***

With this information, you can incorporate these goals into your broader financial plan. The reason that going through this process in such detail is so important is because it forces you to uncover your "why" behind the goal in the first place. When you know your "why," you are far more likely to achieve the goal!

Incorporate Your Goals into Your Plan

In Chapter 2, we discussed a zero-based, three-bucket budget. This method has three main categories: your essentials, your financial goals, and your non-essentials.

We're going to focus on the tactical steps you need to take to break down your SMART financial goals into the broader plan that you create.

STEP 1: The two most important factors in breaking down your goals are that they are Measurable and Timely—meaning you have a dollar amount that you are working toward and a deadline you plan to hit.

TACTICAL STEP: Choose your goal and write down the Measurable and Timely parameters you've defined.

STEP 2: To incorporate these goals into your monthly plan, you now need to break them down into monthly increments. This means you need to do some back-of-the-napkin math to determine your monthly goal target.

TACTICAL STEP: Convert your deadline from years (if applicable) to months. Using our down-payment example, we would convert 3 years to 36 (3 years × 12 months). From there, we take our measurable output ($10,000) and our timely deadline (36 months) and convert it to a monthly figure of $278 ($10,000 over 36 months).

$$3 \times 12 = 36 \qquad \frac{10,000}{36} = \$278$$

STEP 3: Repeat this step for the rest of your financial goals and add up your monthly total. With this total, we can determine how to logically and efficiently factor your financial goals into your plan.

TACTICAL STEP: What percentage of your income goes toward your financial goals? Remember, we are aiming for a 30 percent target, so if your goals are too high of a proportion of your income, to the point where you are unable to pay your expenses, you will need to either prioritize goals one at a time or extend your timeline so the monthly output is lower.

SAVING, INVESTING, AND DEBT PAYOFF

There are three main types of financial goals: savings goals, investing goals, and debt payoff goals. If you are struggling to define where to start, aim to set one goal of each type.

Savings goals: These include any type of short-term savings goal, also called a *sinking fund*. This is a goal that you are saving for incrementally. It is money you plan to use within five years or less. A few examples would be an emergency fund, a vacation fund, or even saving up for a large purchase.

Investing goals: An investing goal is a long-term goal that involves—you guessed it—investing your money (you will learn more about investing in Chapter 5). These could be retirement goals, such as maxing out your 401(k) or an IRA, or general investing using a brokerage account.

Debt payoff goals: These are goals involving paying off or reducing debt balances. They could include student loans, car loans, or even paying off a mortgage over a defined period of time.

Prioritize Your Goals

Your financial goals will likely be a mix of both short-term and long-term goals. It's important to clarify the difference between them as part of the prioritization process.

Short-term goals are those you plan to accomplish within the next five years or less. Some examples include:

- Saving for an emergency fund
- Paying off credit card debt
- Reducing bills by a defined amount
- Saving for a vacation or a wedding
- Going on a spending fast or identifying no-spend categories in your budget
- Purchasing a car

Long-term goals are any goals you plan to accomplish in more than five years, and this is where the majority of your investing goals would fall. Some examples could include:

- Saving for retirement
- Paying off student loans
- Purchasing a home

Once you have your list of goals, you can determine whether they are short-term or long-term goals and use that information to help prioritize them.

ORDER OF OPERATIONS

Prioritization can be difficult, and how you prioritize your goals is ultimately going to be a unique decision based on your own current situation, needs, and desires. There is no specific formula to prioritizing, but there is a general order of operations that may help guide your decision-making.

EMERGENCY FUND

RETIREMENT SAVINGS

DEBT PAYOFF

SHORT-TERM SAVINGS

EMERGENCY SAVINGS

This is the most important financial goal you can set, and it should be your number one priority until you have a full emergency fund. You need to have three months of savings set aside to cover your expenses in case of an emergency. You know your monthly expenses already, so calculating this number is easy!

"*Why*?" You may be wondering. Well, if you were to have some type of emergency, such as unexpectedly losing your job or having an unforeseen medical issue, and you didn't have any savings set aside, you would need to incur debt in order to cover your expenses. This can completely derail your financial progress and make it really hard to climb your way out. Emergency savings are non-negotiable, and until you have them, your other goals are less important.

RETIREMENT SAVINGS

In Chapter 5, I will review why investing early and often is so important, but for now, it's important to know that the earlier you start investing, the more money you can accumulate due to a wonderful concept called *compound interest*.

Retirement savings may be the furthest goal on your mind, because—hello!—retirement is forty-plus years away. That being said, the earlier you start saving, the less you'll actually have to contribute to your retirement savings over time.

If you work a corporate job, you may have a benefit called *Employer Match*. It's a perk that many corporate employers offer their employees when they contribute to their 401(k), which is an employer-sponsored retirement plan (trust me, we'll get there). For example, some employers will offer a 3 percent match to their employees' contributions, meaning if you contribute 3 percent of your salary to your 401(k), your employer will match you, dollar for dollar, up to that 3 percent.

Allocating enough of your income to your 401(k) plan to earn your full employer match is high on this priority list because you are essentially earning free money.

An added benefit is that your contributions can come off the top of your paycheck, so you don't even see them hit your bank account when you get paid. As a result, you learn to live on less and you are saving money without any additional effort.

CONTRIBUTING TO YOUR SAVINGS

A CAVEAT WORTH MENTIONING: Even if your employer doesn't offer a match, contributing 2 to 3 percent of your income to your 401(k) or any retirement account as soon as you can is very important! This allows you to start investing early and doesn't erode your take-home income enough to impact your quality of life.

PAY DOWN HIGH-INTEREST DEBT

High-interest debt is any debt with an interest rate that exceeds 7 percent. This is the threshold because it's close to the historical average return of the stock market, adjusted for inflation. This means that if you have debt that is earning interest *beyond* what you could earn by investing your money, it is worth prioritizing paying it off before making investments (aside from the 2 to 3 percent you're already contributing toward retirement savings).

An example would be credit card debt—which you want to avoid at all costs. If you have already accumulated credit card debt, or any high-interest debt for that matter, don't fret. By prioritizing this goal, you can focus on paying it off as fast as possible, and in the future you can ultimately redirect those funds toward goals that are more exciting.

NOTE: *My favorite debt-payoff strategy is the Avalanche Method (see page 30), which prioritizes your debt based on interest rate. In short, you pay off your debt with the highest interest rate first, which reduces both the amount of interest you pay over time and the time it takes to actually pay it all off.*

FOCUS ON LOW-INTEREST DEBT WHILE SAVING FOR RETIREMENT

Once you've saved an emergency fund, taken advantage of your employer match (if you have one), and paid off any high-interest debt, you can start focusing on paying down low-interest debt while simultaneously saving for retirement.

Low-interest debt would be any debt with an interest rate *below* 7 percent—a great example would be student loans. Student loans can be tricky, especially if you have a hefty amount to pay back. However, prioritizing student loans alongside saving for retirement is an optimal way to reach your long-term goals. First and foremost, you need to make your minimum payment. Minimum debt payments are considered an *essential expense*, so if you're making your minimum payment and don't have additional funds to put toward your loan, that is okay. You're already making progress.

INVESTING

Many college grads will forgo investing until they've paid off their loans, which I personally think is a mistake. If it takes you ten years to pay off your student loans, and you don't start investing for ten years after you graduate college, you've *lost* ten years during which your money could have been growing in the stock market, which can translate to hundreds of thousands of dollars over your lifetime (this will be explained further in Chapter 5).

But if you have the additional wiggle room in your budget, you can increase your monthly student loan payment *and* increase your retirement contribution for a double whammy. This accelerates your loan payoff while allowing your money to earn compound interest as soon as possible.

SAVING BEYOND THE ORDER OF OPERATIONS

It's likely you have financial goals outside of paying off debt and saving for retirement. Where do those fit in? Well, it depends. As I mentioned earlier, there is no formula or equation that you can copy and paste for everyone to use to prioritize goals. It all comes down to *what is important to you*, and, more tactfully, how much disposable income you have.

If you have a lot of additional financial goals, such as saving for a vacation or a wedding, or maybe purchasing a car, and you can't fit them into your plan along with saving for retirement and/or paying off debt, here's what you can do:

1. **FOCUS ON YOUR TIMELINES:** An easy way to reduce the amount of money you are putting toward a financial goal is stretching the timeline. If you have a longer period of time to save for something, the amount you need to save each month is smaller. It's simple math.

2. **FOCUS ON ONE GOAL AT A TIME:** You may not be able to work toward all of your goals at once; that is normal. Choose one, focus on it for a few months or a year or a defined timeline that works for you, and then move on to the next.

Your financial journey is a marathon, not a sprint. You don't need to do everything at once, so give yourself grace and be patient. Plus, often your goals change and shift as you move through life. Keep your mind open to this, as it's likely you'll want to re-evaluate your goals and re-prioritize every few months!

Financial Goals Examples

There are many types of financial goals you can set, as I've discussed throughout this chapter. Here are a few examples of SMART financial goals to help guide your own goal-setting process.

SAVING FOR AN EMERGENCY FUND

SPECIFIC: My goal is to save a three-month emergency fund so that I can have security and peace of mind if I lose my main source of income or if I have a large, unexpected expense come up.

MEASURABLE: I will save $6,000, the equivalent of three months' of my essential expenses.

ACHIEVABLE: I will achieve this goal by opening a high-yield savings account and transferring money every time I get paid, which is twice per month.

RELEVANT: In order to focus on accumulating long-term wealth, I need to save an emergency fund to avoid incurring unexpected financial disaster.

TIMELY: I will save my three-month emergency fund in one year. This means I will set aside $500 per month in order to achieve this goal on time.

FINAL GOAL: My goal is to save a three-month emergency fund—which is $6,000—within one year, so that I can have security and peace of mind if I lose my main source of income or if I have an unexpected large expense come up. I will achieve this goal by opening a high-yield savings account and contributing $500 per month to it. I will transfer $250 every time I get paid, and this will ensure that I have ample money set aside to avoid financial disaster.

CREDIT CARD DEBT PAYOFF

SPECIFIC: I will pay off $5,000 in credit card debt so that I become debt-free and can increase my credit score.

MEASURABLE: I will pay off the $5,000 balance that has a 15 percent Annual Percentage Yield (APY).

ACHIEVABLE: I will achieve this goal by allocating any discretionary money beyond my usual expenses to this balance. I will also stop putting any additional expenses on the card.

RELEVANT: In order to feel financially secure, I need to eliminate my credit card debt and establish a healthy relationship with spending my money.

TIMELY: I will pay off this credit card in one year. This means I will allocate approximately $500 monthly to the balance.

FINAL GOAL: My goal is to pay off my entire credit card balance—which is $5,000—in one year so that I can become debt-free and increase my credit score. I will do this by allocating any additional discretionary income beyond my usual expenses to this balance, and I will stop putting any expenses on the card. Paying off this debt will help me feel financially secure and establish a healthy relationship with spending my money.

SAVING FOR A VACATION

SPECIFIC: My goal is to save enough for a one-week vacation at an all-inclusive resort in the Bahamas with my partner. I will pay for the vacation in full.

MEASURABLE: The entire vacation, accounting for flights, airport transportation, hotel, and activities is $6,000. If I use credit-card points for the flights, the total out-of-pocket cost is $4,500.

ACHIEVABLE: I will achieve this goal by utilizing credit-card points for our flights and ensuring that I have a high-yield savings account to keep my vacation savings separate from money intended for my other goals.

RELEVANT: This vacation will be a simultaneous celebration of our anniversary and birthdays over the last year. It will be a chance to unplug, relax, and recharge from our daily lives.

TIMELY: We want to go on this vacation during the holidays in one year. I will save $750 per month for the next six months so I can book the vacation in advance and pay in full.

FINAL GOAL: My goal is to save enough for a one-week, all-inclusive vacation in the Bahamas during the holidays next year with my partner. If I utilize credit-card points for our flights, I will need to save $4,500 within the next six months so that I can book the vacation in advance and pay in full. I will do this by saving $750 per month in a high-yield savings account to keep these savings separate from my money intended for other goals.

PAYING OFF STUDENT LOANS

SPECIFIC: I want to pay off my entire federal student loan balance so that I can become debt-free by my thirtieth birthday. I am currently twenty-four years old.

MEASURABLE: My entire balance is $30,000 and the interest rate is 3 percent. My minimum monthly payment is $290.

ACHIEVABLE: I will achieve this by incorporating my minimum payment into my essential expenses every month and then allocating an additional 10 percent of my take-home pay toward paying the balance.

RELEVANT: I want to pay off my student loans in my twenties so that I can enter my thirties entirely debt-free. This will allow me to feel financially confident and focus on building long-term wealth.

TIMELY: I will pay off this balance in six years, by my thirtieth birthday. This means I will pay my $290 minimum every month, plus an additional $150 to accelerate the payoff timeline.

FINAL GOAL: I will pay off my entire federal student loan balance, which is $30,000, by the time I turn thirty. I am twenty-four right now. To accomplish this goal within six years, I will pay the minimum payment of $290 per month, plus an additional $150 monthly to accelerate the timeline. Paying off my student loans before my thirties will help me feel financially confident so that I can enter a new decade debt-free.

CHAPTER 3 MONEY REVIEW

Financial goals provide you with a sense of direction: They define the path you are on and enable you to create a financial roadmap to achieve them. Without a goal, it is difficult to create any type of financial plan.

The best way to set financial goals is to make them SMART: This means the goal is specific, measurable, achievable, relevant, and timely. By using this method, you can get crystal clear on exactly what you hope to accomplish and then break the goal down into digestible steps within your plan.

Breaking down your goals into your plan is a three-step process: First, highlight the measurable and timely aspects of each financial goal. Then, divide the measurable amount you've defined by the number of months it will take you to reach it. The final step is to incorporate this monthly number into your zero-based, three-bucket budget.

There are three types of financial goals you can work toward: The three types are savings goals, investing goals, and debt payoff goals. An ideal scenario is working toward one of each at any given time. You do not need to silo yourself into only working toward one goal—unless you have credit card debt!

When prioritizing your goals, you'll want to follow an order of operations: Your emergency fund is the highest priority, followed by paying off credit card debt. Once you've accomplished both of those, you can move on to investing for retirement, saving for short-term goals, and paying off low-interest debt. There are a few caveats along the way—such as taking advantage of a 401(k) match, for example.

There is no one-size-fits-all solution: How you prioritize is determined by your income, the goals you've already accomplished, and what is most important to you. Setting goals and getting clear on your *why* is what will inform how you prioritize your various goals within the general order of operations.

CHAPTER 3 ACTION ITEMS

Set three to five SMART financial goals: They can be savings, investing, or debt payoff goals. You can use the goal-setting worksheet provided on page 167 to guide you through this process.

Prioritize your goals based on the order of operations: Once you've set your SMART goals, rank them in order of priority. By doing so, you can build your goals into your plan based on what is most important to you. If you need to choose a few goals to work on at a time, you can follow your order of operations. If you come into additional income, you can distribute it based on this ranking.

Break your goals down into monthly increments: By considering the measurable and timely aspects of each goal, you can break it down into a monthly amount to build into your plan. You can do this on the goals worksheet that is provided.

Chapter Four

Spend Your Money on Things That Matter

....

Why don't we ever learn how to spend our money? Conventional financial advice focuses on how to save, but rarely on how to spend. Early on in my career, I went to a conference at which a speaker said something that has stuck with me to this day: "Stop spending your money on your friends' hobbies."

It sounds so obvious and straightforward. Yet it was something that I had never thought about before: I was spending money on my friends' interests *all the time*, and mostly out of social pressure. The example the speaker used is one that resonated with me as well: going to a boozy brunch with friends just about every weekend. It wasn't enjoyable to me because it was expensive and often involved over-indulging (and thus feeling worse later both financially and physically!).

Now, if you love those types of brunches, great—you will have no problem allocating money to them. However, for those who feel similarly to me, the underlying "goal" of going to brunch isn't the alcohol or the food; it is to see friends. There are other ways you can fill that need in your life without spending money.

How many times have you spent money on activities your *friends* wanted to do? One of the strongest pressures in the world is social pressure—and learning how to say "no" is an art many people haven't mastered. This means most people don't use their money in a way that is aligned with *their* values and priorities. Instead, they spend money out of pressure, on things they don't care about, to make other people happy before themselves.

It's outrageous! But saying no, especially because you don't want to spend money, can feel even worse. So, what's the solution?

....

Stop Spending Money on Sh*t You Don't Care About

At the time of this writing, did you know that more than half of "upper-income" Americans are living paycheck to paycheck? Bad spending habits can derail your financial plan no matter your income. And the effects can be not only painful, but devastating—whether that's paying thousands of additional dollars in interest or not being able to cover an emergency expense and thus incurring credit card debt.

Beyond that, poor money habits can ruin your life. Poor credit and a lack of savings can block you from realizing your long-term goals—from buying a house to retiring at a reasonable age. The silver lining? Habits can be changed. But to better understand how to change your habits, you first need to identify what habits could be derailing your financial success. Here are five of the most common negative spending habits.

1. OVERSPENDING

Overspending is defined as spending beyond one's means. Usually, this has less to do with an inability to pay your bills and more to do with making suboptimal spending decisions on a regular basis.

It is the most common negative spending habit that people deal with, and it's been amplified by advertisements infiltrating your life. Between seeing thousands of ads per day and the ability to simply "tap to purchase" directly within an app, it's no wonder overspending is so common!

Social pressure contributes to overspending as well, especially for young people. It can be hard to say no to a dinner out, a vacation, or the latest shopping trend (especially when you see your peers on social media enjoying all of these experiences). People think spending money makes you happy. Although this may be true in certain instances, spending more than you can afford does just the opposite.

2. TREATING YOUR CREDIT CARD LIKE FREE MONEY

Not to be dramatic, but credit card debt will ruin your life. Seriously. Credit cards have the highest interest rates of any form of debt—with some running all the way up to 20 percent annually.

The long-term financial implications of incurring credit card debt are hard to escape. Many credit cards charge compounding interest, meaning if you don't pay your statement in full each billing month, interest is continually added onto the balance that you are also paying interest on.

It's important to keep in mind that credit card interest compounds even if you make the minimum payment each month—and this is why you need to pay the balance off completely.

Your credit card is not free money. If you don't have the money to pay off each purchase you make on your card the moment you swipe it, then you can't afford to make the purchase.

3. EMOTIONAL SHOPPING

Emotional spending happens when you spend your money during a period of—you guessed it—heightened emotions. This is very common, especially when you're sad, stressed, or anxious. It often results in you buying items you don't really want or didn't need in the first place.

The reason so many people do this is because when you make a purchase your brain releases both endorphins and dopamine. This gives you a rush. It can literally make you feel better, which can lead to you using shopping as a coping mechanism.

This can take you down a dark path, such as overspending or credit card debt. It becomes problematic when it happens often, or when you are buying things that are completely out of character and misaligned with your values and priorities.

4. LIFESTYLE INFLATION

Lifestyle inflation is when you increase your spending as you increase your income. It often happens when you get a new job or a raise at work. You're making more money, so you think "It's time to upgrade my apartment," or, "Now I can afford a nicer car."

As a result, you're unable to improve your financial situation because any additional money you make is going toward more and more stuff, whether it's tangible or not. That additional income *isn't* going toward savings, investments, or paying off debt, and you end up spinning the wheel in the same place instead of moving the needle forward.

In the long term, lifestyle inflation can derail your financial future, especially if you are funding a lifestyle you can no longer afford.

5. AVOIDANCE

Avoidance happens when you completely avoid your financial situation. You don't pay attention to how much money you're spending, you don't look at your credit card statement, and you can't remember the last time you checked your savings account balance.

Logging into your credit card account to see a month's worth of charges or checking your bank account after you paid rent to see that the balance is ebbing closer and closer to zero isn't a great feeling. To avoid that feeling, you might even avoid looking. This can be so uncomfortable that you avoid your finances entirely, resulting in a snowballing situation that can keep you stuck in a negative cycle for years.

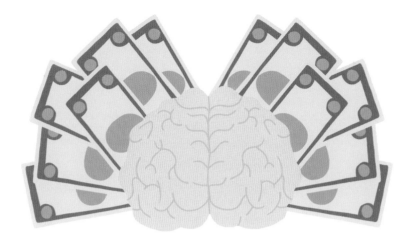

The Benefits of Conscious Spending

If you're feeling seen because of one or more of those detrimental spending habits that I've described, you're probably wondering what you can do about it. The solution is a fun term called *conscious spending*. This is the spending principle I live by, and it will change your life.

Simply put, conscious spending is exactly what it sounds like: being conscious when you spend your money. It means that you pay attention to how you're spending, where you're spending, and to all of your day-to-day spending decisions.

The mission behind this is that you take time to get to know yourself, your goals, and what you want out of life. Then, armed with this information, you can make more mindful decisions, using your money as a tool for living the life you want.

Conscious spending will change the way you use your money. I'm going to share some of the key benefits.

1. YOU DON'T HAVE TO FOCUS ON SPENDING LESS MONEY

The entire premise of conscious spending isn't necessarily about *spending less*, it's about *spending better*. Often, when you think about building a budget, organizing your finances, and improving your money situation, you probably also think about cutting expenses and avoiding spending money.

Pull up your credit card or debit card statement for the last three months and comb through your expenses. Which of these expenses do you actually remember? Which made you feel really good? Which have you completely forgotten about, or make you feel guilty or icky?

Take note of each response and start to group them together. Do you notice any patterns? Maybe you've spent a lot of money going out to restaurants, but through spending on going out to eat you've also created a ton of amazing memories with your friends or partner, and that makes you feel really happy inside. Or maybe you've spent a ton of money on delivery and weren't even aware of it. This makes you feel guilty and uncomfortable, and now you realize that you want to spend your money differently.

The goal is to start focusing your spending on the things that give you a positive feeling when you think back to them and to reduce your spending on the things that make you feel bad.

> NOTE: *If you feel guilty when you buy something, try this: Every time you make a purchase, invest or save the same amount. That way, the next time you splurge, you're also investing for your future.*

2. YOU CAN BUY THINGS YOU ACTUALLY WANT

Have you ever felt like you don't have enough money to go on your dream vacation or splurge on that new pair of sneakers you've been eyeing for months? Well, odds are you actually do have the money. You're just spending it on sh*t you don't care about.

By implementing conscious spending, you can redirect your money to purchases that actually make you happy. This means spending less money on things that don't make you feel good—like brunch, if you think back to the introduction of this chapter—and using that money instead on things that *do* make you feel good.

MY CONSCIOUS SPENDING DECISIONS

Conscious spending changed my life. I've been following this method for a few years now, and I have a very intimate relationship with how I spend my money and what I spend it on to feel my best. Here are a few examples of how I implement conscious spending in my own life:

Coffee: I'm not just talking about buying coffee at my local shop. I mean that I take my morning coffee very seriously, and I've invested my own money into this as a result. I splurged on a Nespresso coffee maker, and I spend a hefty chunk of change every few months to buy the pods that I love, which are $1.40 apiece. Could I buy a coffee pot and grind my own beans to keep my morning cup at 30 cents? Yeah, but I don't want to. My morning coffee dictates my entire day. If it isn't how I like it, my day is ruined. To you, that might sound dramatic. But to me, it's the difference between a productive day and a grumpy day. If the extra dollar means I'm having a good day, it's worth it.

Eating out: I'll admit it—I love to go out to eat. I love being waited on, cleaned up after, and enjoying an amazing meal with friends or family. And I'm willing to spend money on it. When I go out to eat, I also love to order whatever I want. This means ordering the appetizers, a second glass of wine, and even dessert if I'm feeling crazy. Because of this, I prioritize my eating-out spending on *eating out*. I very rarely order takeout, and you'll *never* catch me ordering Uber Eats or DoorDash. If I'm going to spend money on food, it's out at a restaurant, not on lukewarm takeout that I eat on the couch.

Exercise: Here's an example of how my conscious spending decisions have changed and evolved with my life. A few years ago, while I was living in Boston, I would spend $150 a month on a luxury gym. I love working out, and this gym was next to my office, it had clean equipment, clean showers, and a steam room. But when the global pandemic hit and the gym closed, I needed to reevaluate my exercise regimen. During that period, I fell in love with Pilates and subscribed to an online platform that cost me $20 a month. And since then, I've decided that spending $150 is no longer worth it for me because I love doing at-home Pilates. Now, I spend that $20 monthly for the subscription, and I've repurposed the money I am saving from a gym membership on other things. It's normal for your priorities to change, and your spending should change with them.

Part of being a conscious spender is identifying why you spend money on things that don't bring value into your life. With this information, you can fill that void with other purchases or experiences.

Using the brunch example, going to brunch wasn't about the food for me, it was about spending time with friends! But there are many other ways to spend time with friends and get the same feeling without spending $100 on something you don't like.

3. YOU WILL HAVE MONEY TO FUND YOUR GOALS

You could be thinking, "If I am spending all this money on the things I love, how will I be able to reach my goals?"

With conscious spending, you aren't necessarily spending *more* on non-essentials than you would otherwise, you're simply spending *better*—meaning you are spending more of your discretionary income on the things you love and less on the things you don't.

This doesn't (and shouldn't) impact the money you set aside for your financial goals. The principles we discussed in earlier chapters about prioritizing your goals don't change.

The benefit is that you can now spend money on things you enjoy *and* reach your goals. Sounds amazing, right? It is.

SPENDING MONEY AS A HABIT

Humans are creatures of habit, and it's likely you spend money on things that you aren't even thinking about because you associate them with a certain activity or because they are ingrained in your regular routine.

Think through your day-to-day: Are there any patterns that come to mind? It could be buying something just because it's on sale, or maybe it's increasing your online shopping cart to get free shipping (guilty!). Or it could be ignoring purchases because they're "only a few dollars"—these are called *microtransactions,* and they can add up if you don't pay attention to them.

One of the goals of conscious spending is to bring attention to these habits and start changing your behavior. Every swipe, every purchase, and every transaction should be thought through. Eventually, your spending will feel really natural and you won't have to pay attention to it as closely.

THE ART OF SAYING NO

The beauty of conscious spending is that it determines what you will and will not spend money on. Saying no can be hard, especially with social pressure, peer pressure, and the pressure to keep up with the Kardashians (no pun intended).

Society today is incredibly materialistic, and this is flaunted all over the social media that you consume daily, inundating you with new products and experiences that are easily accessible with the tap of your finger. But as a conscious spender, you've learned the art of saying no. You've decided what will and will not add value to your life, and thus you've decided what you will and will not spend money on.

The hard part is sticking to it; this means getting comfortable with turning things down if they don't serve you, or maybe saying "no" to that friend who consistently pressures you into doing things with them that involve spending money you don't want to spend.

Saying no is an art. It comes down to setting boundaries and sticking to your values and goals, knowing that every decision you make is bringing you one step closer to the life you want to live.

4. YOU WILL FEEL MORE FINANCIALLY CONFIDENT

Feeling confident about how you use your money translates into feeling more confident with your finances as a whole. If you feel more confident with your finances, you will make better financial decisions on a consistent basis. You'll also feel less stressed and anxious about your money, which will help you to show up as a better version of yourself in other areas of your life.

Your finances permeate your entire life: They dictate where you can afford to live, activities you can afford to do, and decisions you can afford to make—such as not staying in a job you hate because you need the money. Don't underestimate the power of financial confidence and confident spending. You'll soon realize that using your money as a tool to enhance your life will change your entire perspective.

CHAPTER 4 MONEY REVIEW

Bad spending habits can ruin your financial life: Whether it's overspending, treating a credit card like free money, emotional shopping, lifestyle inflation, or avoidance, a poor spending habit can block you from reaching your financial goals.

Conscious spending will change the way you approach your money: Taking an intentional approach to your spending patterns, incorporating your values into your financial decisions, and aligning your day-to-day spending with your long-term goals will transform your ability to save money.

Spending intentionally has a ton of intangible benefits: It takes the focus away from spending less and shifts it to spending *more* on the things that add value to your life. Plus, it enables you to feel more financially confident and free up discretionary income to put toward your goals.

Learning how to say no is an art: Your superpower is learning how to say no to items, experiences, and plans that won't add value to your life. It can be hard to turn things down, especially with peer pressure and the fear of potentially disappointing your friends. Ultimately, becoming comfortable with your financial boundaries will set you free.

CHAPTER 4 ACTION ITEMS

Review your spending from the last three to six months: Pull up your transactions and comb through all of your expenses as of late. What transactions do you recall being really fun or adding value to your life? Are there any that you completely forgot about, or that now, looking back, you regret spending money on? Identify which you'd like to continue spending money on and which you can do without.

Identify value categories for your spending: Now that you've reviewed your transactions, what patterns do you notice? Are the expenses that added value to your life concentrated within certain areas of your budget, such as travel or going out to eat? Are the expenses that you regret or don't feel excited about similar in type? Categorize them and identify some themes around your spending.

Revisit your non-essential budget: Now that you understand conscious spending, go back and review the non-essential spending categories that you outlined in previous chapters. Are there changes you'd like to make and implement going forward? How can you adjust your budget to better reflect your conscious spending themes?

Investing? Never Heard of Her

When I was younger, the idea of investing freaked me out. I learned about it in college through my coursework and various internships, so I knew it was important, but it took a long time for me to get started. I was investing through my 401(k) at work, but anything beyond that scared me.

It always felt like a complicated boys' club that was designed to scare people away if they didn't understand the jargon. I had this idea in my head that it was too hard, the concepts were too confusing, and I needed to leave it up to someone else to do it for me because I wasn't smart enough to do it on my own.

In fact, for a time after I graduated college, I had a financial advisor. And although she was excellent, after some self-education and a little on-the-job training, I realized it was unnecessary for me to keep seeing her. In my various jobs post-grad, I was exposed to different opportunities during which I learned about asset allocation, portfolio construction, and investment research for large institutions.

Although this is very different from investing related to personal finances, it gave me enough exposure to understand how to make investment decisions, how to evaluate different investments, and how to weigh different investment options against each other. Over time, I realized that I could apply what I was learning in my job to my real life, and that is where the fun began!

I know that not everyone is able to learn about investing at school and at work, and because of this, many people are paralyzed when it comes to investing their money and understanding why it's so important to start doing so as soon as possible. My goal is to demystify investing and make it as simple as I can.

Like any new concept, investing is a lot to learn up front, and that can feel overwhelming. I encourage you to take your time and be open to a little discomfort, knowing that ultimately you can use what you learn to set the foundation for your investment strategy over the course of your lifetime!

Saving Isn't Enough

If you're reading this book, you know that you need to invest. Investing allows you to put your money to work—but what does that even mean? Here's an example to help illustrate this concept.

Imagine you just graduated college and you land a solid job making $75,000 per year. On your first day of work, you meet your peer—let's call her Michelle—who is working the same role and making the same amount of money as you are. Objectively, you are complete equals.

You instantly become friends and find yourself chatting about your budget and financial goals over lunch later that week. Michelle tells you that she already set up her 401(k) and she is contributing 15 percent of her salary to it every paycheck. This is about $400 every pay period.

You think to yourself, "*fifteen* percent?! How can she afford that?" But instead of expressing your disbelief, you smile and nod, because not only do you have no idea how to open up a 401(k), you know there's a better chance of seeing God in the flesh than parting with $400 every two weeks.

A year goes by, and as you and Michelle are celebrating your one-year work anniversary, she mentions that she has almost $12,000 in her 401(k). You practically spit out your lunch—"*Twelve THOUSAND dollars?! How is that even possible?*" The wheels in your brain start turning, trying to figure out how that could be.

After running some quick numbers, you realize that they do, in fact, add up. "*Wow, in one year she has $12,000 in her 401(k), and I have zero. I need to start saving.*"

On that day, you decide that you'll put $200 per paycheck into a savings account. What you don't account for is the difference between a *savings account* and a *401(k)*. With a savings account, your money has no opportunity to grow; it just sits in the account until you decide to withdraw it. With a 401(k), you are investing your money in the stock market, and as a result it's growing in value over time, earning *compound interest*.

A couple years later, after both you and Michelle have gone your separate ways, you run into her and grab lunch together. She tells you that she's kept up with her 401(k) at her new job, and in the five years since she started, she has nearly $70,000.

This blows your mind, because you've been saving, too, by putting $200 per month into your savings account. But you only have $12,000—how does she have so much more?

The answer is compound interest. Compound interest is the concept of earning interest on both the principal value of your money (what you have invested), as well as the interest you've earned on those investments. It's a lot easier to just show you the numbers, so let's do some math!

COMPOUND INTEREST: THE EIGHTH WONDER OF THE WORLD

Okay, so in this example, Michelle decided to invest $400 per pay period (every two weeks) into her 401(k), meaning that she is investing $10,400 every year. She started doing this in her first job—at age twenty-two—right after she graduated college.

Assuming she maintains this pace for the duration of her working life, she would retire at age sixty-five with nearly $2.6 million*. You read that right—$2.6 MILLION.

This is the result of compound interest—every year she earns interest on top of a higher and higher value. As a result, her money grows exponentially, as seen in the graph below:

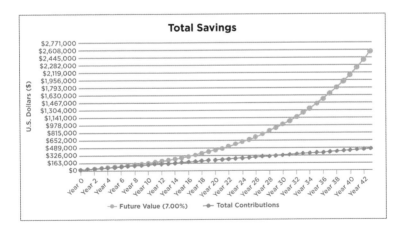

*The average historical return on the U.S. stock market is 10 percent annually. Keeping in mind that inflation reduces purchasing power by 2 to 3 percent each year, we land at a 7 percent return assumption. Remember, this is an assumption for illustrative purposes only and is not a guarantee.

Now, let's pivot to your situation. You decided to save your money instead of learning how to open up a 401(k) at work. Every pay period for the duration of your working life, you save $200 into a regular savings account. This works out to be $5,200 per year.

Keep in mind, you started at age twenty-three, because for your first year out of college, you didn't save anything. Assuming you maintain this pace, by the time you turn sixty-five and are ready to retire, you will have saved $218,400.

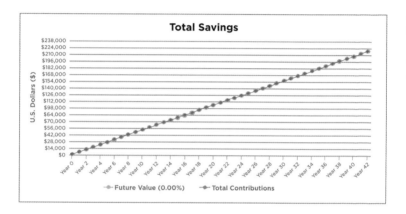

Let me be clear: This is by no means a small chunk of change, as it's well over $200,000! However, it is minuscule compared to Michelle's savings. In fact, it's more than $2 MILLION less.

And the difference isn't a result of you landing on $200 per paycheck while she landed on $400. If you had saved $400 instead, you'd have $436,800. Again, that is a lot of money, but it's still $2 million less than Michelle made over the same period of time.

The key difference between these two examples is saving versus investing. When you put your money into a savings account, it has no opportunity to grow and earn compound interest. When you invest your money—for example, using a 401(k) (we'll get into the details of this account type later on in this chapter)—your money has the opportunity to grow exponentially.

Now imagine a few years later on your thirty-fifth birthday, you decide you're going to start investing that $200 and open up a 401(k) rather than put it into a savings account. You do exactly what Michelle does and maintain this pace for thirty years until you retire at sixty-five.

At sixty-five, you retire with $491,000. You think, "I should have done $400 per pay period instead of $200 and I'd have way more money. How did Michelle end up with so much more?"

I hate to be the bearer of bad news, but even if you had upped the ante to $400, you still wouldn't crack $1 million by retirement. In fact, you'd retire with around $982,000.*

The reason? TIME. As a refresher, Michelle started putting that $400 into her 401(k) as soon as she started working, at age twenty-two. This means her money had forty-three years to accumulate and grow.

By waiting just a few years—in your imaginary case, you waited thirteen years before you started investing in your 401(k)—you lost out on precious time in the market for your money to grow. As a result, even by investing the same amount as Michelle, you were never able to catch up.

If you were to invest twice as much as Michelle—let's say at age thirty-five you start investing a whopping $800 per pay period, or $20,800 per year—you still would not catch up. In fact, you'd retire with $1.9 million*, which is nearly $700,000 less than Michelle.

The lesson here? Be like Michelle. Michelle invested early and often, resulting in a slow but steady accumulation of wealth. Worry less about how much and more about how early you can start.

This illustration is not meant to scare you or make you feel behind. It's meant to show you just how important TIME in the market is, and that the earlier you start, the less you'll need to invest to earn more. Understanding this concept, and the math behind it, can change your financial future. And if you're older than twenty-two, or feel like you're getting a late start, I understand your frustration by seeing these numbers.

Unfortunately, the math is the math, and the numbers don't lie. That being said, you can use this information to empower your decision-making going forward. The best time to start investing was yesterday. The second-best time to start investing is right now.

*The average historical return on the U.S. stock market is 10 percent annually. Keeping in mind that inflation reduces purchasing power by 2 to 3 percent each year, we land at a 7 percent return assumption. Remember, this is an assumption for illustrative purposes only and is not a guarantee.

Set Yourself Up to Invest

Now that I have sufficiently scared you into investing ASAP, I'm going to walk you through the different account types you have to choose from, following my Investment Prioritization System (IPS). This system builds on itself, so once you have the first layer mastered, you can move on to the next and beyond.

With an IPS, you can optimize your accounts to ensure you're taking advantage of opportunities that your workplace may provide, along with tax benefits so that you can keep more of your hard-earned money in your own pocket, as opposed to forking it over in taxes.

LAYER 1: EMPLOYER 401(K) + MATCH

A 401(k) is an employer-sponsored retirement plan by which an employee can contribute a percentage of their income directly to an investment account. Retirement accounts—including 401(k)s—offer you a deal. Essentially, you contribute money to it and reap a tax benefit, either today or when you retire, depending on your account type. This means you reduce your tax obligation and keep more money in your pocket.

Depending on your employer, you may have the option to choose between a Roth 401(k) and a Traditional 401(k). The main difference between these two options is the timing of when you reap that tax benefit.

ROTH VS. TRADITIONAL ACCOUNTS

There are two main types of tax-advantaged retirement accounts, and they are applicable to either a 401(k) retirement plan or an IRA—an Individual Retirement Account. There are a few key differences between them, but the main one is the timing of the tax benefit.

TRADITIONAL: With a traditional 401(k) or IRA, you contribute pre-tax dollars to the account. As a result, your taxable income is reduced by the amount you contribute, and you reap the tax benefit *today*. When you withdraw money from these accounts at retirement, you will pay taxes on the withdrawals.

ROTH: With a Roth 401(k) or IRA, you contribute post-tax dollars to the account. As a result, there is no tax benefit in the year you contribute, but you are able to withdraw the funds tax-free when you retire. An important note to make about a Roth IRA is that there are income limits. This means if you earn beyond a certain threshold in income, you are not eligible for this type of account. These limits change annually, so be sure to look up the limit in the year you are reading this book.

In some instances, your employer may offer a "401(k) match," meaning they will match your contribution up to a certain percentage. If this option is provided to you, take full advantage and contribute up to the match at a minimum.

For example, let's say you make $50,000 and your employer will match 100 percent of your contributions up to 3 percent of your salary. This means you'd contribute $1,500, and your employer would contribute $1,500. This is free money—take it!

Given there are so many advantages to a 401(k)—specifically related to the tax benefits—there are also certain restrictions that come along with it, primarily focused on contribution limits. With a 401(k), regardless of whether you open a Roth or Traditional, you are limited in how much you can contribute to it. As of 2022, the 401(k) contribution limit is $20,500—meaning in the 2022 tax year you can only contribute up to that amount (not including your employer match). These limits change often, so be sure to look up what the limits are in the year that you are reading this book.

A 401(K) MATCH: WHAT'S THE CATCH?

Having an employer 401(k) match is an amazing benefit, but with every benefit, sometimes there is a catch. In this case, the catch is what is called *vesting*. Every employer has a different vesting schedule and policy, so if you're unsure what yours is, reach out to an HR contact at your company.

A vesting schedule is an incentive schedule that is determined by your employer; it is the employer's way of giving you a reason to stay with the company. The way this works is by "vesting" employer contributions to your 401(k) over a period of time. If you leave the company before the contributions are fully vested, you are only entitled to the portion that has been vested based on your tenure at the company.

Vesting does not apply to contributions you've made; that money belongs to you. But the contributions your employer makes (your employer match) could be bound to a vesting schedule. The longer you work at a company, the more the company's contributions vest and belong to you. It sounds confusing, so let's look at an example.

Imagine your company follows a five-year vesting schedule, and every year your 401(k) contributions vest 20 percent. In year one, you are entitled to 20 percent of the employer match provided to you. In year two, that 20 percent increases to 40 percent, in year three it increases to 60 percent, and so on up until your fifth work anniversary, when the contributions become 100 percent vested.

If your employer matched your 401(k) contributions up to 3 percent of your $50k salary, thus matching your $1,500 contribution, and you left the company after one year, you'd only be entitled to 20 percent of that $1,500 that they matched. You keep your $1,500 contribution and walk away with $300 of their contribution.

This is important to grasp, especially when making a decision to leave your job. If you aren't aware of your employer's vesting schedule, use this as a sign to look it up!

When you think about it—contribution limits aside—a 401(k) is a pretty awesome investment account type. You get a tax benefit, often your employer offers a match, and you can invest automatically. If you have a 401(k) available to you, use it!

> NOTE: *What does it mean to "max out" your 401(k)? Since retirement accounts such as 401(k)s and IRAs have contribution limits, the goal is to contribute as much as you can to these accounts in order to maximize your tax benefit each calendar year. When you have contributed the maximum amount to either, it's referred to as* maxing out *your 401(k) or IRA.*

LAYER 2: INDIVIDUAL RETIREMENT ACCOUNT (IRA)

This is another type of retirement account. Like a 401(k), this account is designed to incentivize saving for retirement and reaping tax benefits. Unlike a 401(k), it is not linked to your employer, so any individual can open an IRA.

You have two options when opening an IRA: a Roth or a Traditional. These different account types have different parameters related to income limits, contribution limits, withdrawal penalties, and more. The IRS loves to complicate everything, so these limits change every year. To understand which you qualify for based on the year you read this book, you can look up "Roth and Traditional IRA Limits" at www.IRS.gov.

Opening an IRA is fairly straightforward, and I'm going to walk you through the steps in detail:

1. **CHOOSE YOUR BROKERAGE.** A brokerage is essentially the "middleman" that connects you—the investor—to the stocks or funds you want to buy. There are tons of brokerages to choose from, but a couple that I personally like are Vanguard and Fidelity, because they tend to offer many investment options with low fees, and they have great customer service departments.

2. **OPEN UP THE ACCOUNT.** You can usually do this right on the brokerage website, and they will walk you through it step by step. Generally, this process should take about thirty minutes to an hour and will require you to enter your social security number, bank account numbers, and other personal information. Make sure to have this readily available to speed up the process. If you find yourself lost, you can always call their customer service line and have someone help you open it over the phone.

SHOULD I MAX OUT MY 401(K) OR IRA FIRST?

When saving for retirement, there are so many options that it can be difficult to strategize and prioritize the different accounts. The general rule of thumb is as follows:

First, contribute to your 401(k) up to the employer match, if you have one. If your employer offers a match, it is *free money*, so take it! For example, if your employer matches 100 percent of your contributions up to 3 percent of your salary, then set your 401(k) contributions to 3 percent at a minimum to get the full match.

Second, pivot your focus to maxing out your Roth IRA, if you have one. As I mentioned earlier, Roth IRAs have restrictions, one of which is an income limit. Be sure to check the limits in the year you are reading this book.

The reason I suggest pivoting to an IRA rather than maintaining focus on your 401(k) is because of fees. Many 401(k)s have management fees that are outside of your control—it depends on the brokerage that your employer chooses and the investment options available to you. Most IRAs do not have any management fees, and the only fees you'll pay are those associated with the investment funds you choose. There are many low- or no-fee funds that you can choose from.

Finally, if you've contributed up to your employer match and also maxed out your IRA, then you can refocus back on your 401(k). Aim to max out your IRA and 401(k) before moving on to a taxable investment account if your goal is to take advantage of as many tax benefits as possible.

3. **CHOOSE YOUR INVESTMENTS.** Later in this chapter, I will give you an overview of different investment types, but the most important takeaway to remember in this process is that you *have to invest the money*. A very common mistake people make after opening their IRA is transferring the money into a settlement account—which is just a cash account to hold your dollars—and not actually buying the investments. *You must purchase investments within your IRA!*

Don't let the set-up process intimidate you. Once you have the account set up, it's very easy to maintain. You can set up auto-investments as well, making the entire process mindless!

LAYER 3: TAXABLE INVESTMENT ACCOUNT

A taxable investment account is called a *brokerage account*. This type of investment account has no tax benefits, meaning you will contribute income that has already been taxed, and when you sell your investments and withdraw the money, you will pay capital gains tax on it. The benefit of a taxable brokerage account is that you have access to the money whenever you need it, whereas with retirement accounts such as 401(k)s and IRAs, there are penalties associated with withdrawing the money before age 59½.

Once you've maxed out your 401(k) and IRA, you can move on to investing with a brokerage account. You can open a brokerage account with the same broker you used to open an IRA, and I recommend doing this because it can help keep your accounts organized and consolidated in one place.

OPTIMIZE YOUR STRATEGY WITH AUTOMATION

Once you have all your accounts set up, you can start feeding them through automatic investments. With a 401(k), your contributions are automatically deducted from your paycheck, and after you've enrolled you don't need to do much else unless you choose to increase or decrease your contribution.

With an IRA and a brokerage account, you can set up an automatic investment schedule on a set cadence of your choice. Automating your investments will make it a lot easier to stick to a schedule and ultimately spend less time getting better results.

Investment Types

I want to make investing as simple and straightforward as possible from the beginning, so I am going to explain to you the basics of the different investment types. With this information, you can decide how hands on or hands off you want to be when building your investment portfolio.

I like to use what I call the Flower Shop Analogy to make it easier to conceptualize these different investment types.

STOCKS: AN INDIVIDUAL FLOWER

A stock is part ownership in a company. Essentially, when you purchase a stock, you are purchasing part of a company, and as a result a share in the company's profits. Purchasing a stock is like walking into a flower shop and buying a single flower; there are many to choose from, some more appealing than others due to their different attributes. When you choose one, based on the type of flower you've selected, you may have an idea of how long it will live, but its lifespan is also dependent on the care you provide for it and the environment you put it in.

Similarly to buying a single flower from a flower shop, you can choose a single stock to purchase. There are so many to choose from across various industries, and some may be more appealing than others—for example, a tech stock might seem more promising than a tobacco stock in the twenty-first century. Based on your research, you may have an idea of how a stock might perform over time, but there are so many factors beyond your control that may dictate if it provides a high return (or blooms like a beautiful flower) or results in you losing money (like a shriveled-up flower).

MUTUAL FUND: A FANCY FLORAL ARRANGEMENT

A mutual fund is a pool of money that is used to purchase a basket of stocks. Simply put, individuals will decide on the type of fund that would suit them—it could be based on company size, industry, or geographic location, to name a few—and hand their money over to an investment manager (a trained professional) who will choose the stocks to invest in on their behalf. These are popular because they allow you to invest in multiple stocks at once, which allows for diversification.

Going back to the Flower Shop Analogy, think of a mutual fund like a fancy floral arrangement that you order. You're not a flower expert, so you want to leave it up to the professionals to create an arrangement for you based on the type of flowers you're looking for. You order ahead, give them your money, and leave it up to them to choose the flowers for you. This way, you get a wide array of flowers that all fit together nicely.

ETF (EXCHANGE TRADED FUND): A BOUQUET

An ETF, or Exchange Traded Fund, is a hybrid between an individual stock and a mutual fund, as it has attributes of both. Similarly to a stock, an ETF trades on what's called an *exchange*—this is just the marketplace where individuals and brokers buy and sell stocks. Similarly to a mutual fund, with an ETF you are purchasing a basket of stocks that have some type of commonality or theme.

Using the Flower Shop Analogy, an ETF would be a bouquet. You're getting a variety of different flowers arranged based on a similar type, so they all fit together nicely, but it's much easier and more convenient to purchase a bouquet—you can just walk into the store and choose one, rather than needing to order ahead for a fancy flower arrangement.

DEFINING DIVERSIFICATION

Have you ever heard the phrase "Don't put all your eggs in one basket"? The meaning behind it is a warning to not put all of your resources into one area, as you run the risk of losing everything. This is a very important concept when it comes to investing, and it's called *diversification*.

Every investment involves some degree of risk—there is no such thing as a "risk-free" investment. If you ever hear someone telling you they can generate a return for you risk-free, it's a scam, and they are lying to you!

If you were to choose one specific stock and invest 100 percent of your money in it, you'd run the risk of losing your life's savings. Let's say that company went out of business; any money you invested into it would be gone.

But if you were to invest in ten different companies, with 10 percent of your money going to each, and one company went out of business but the other companies performed really well, you'd only lose 10 percent of your money. The other 90 percent was spread across other companies.

The true reason you need to diversify your investments is to manage the risk associated with investing. If you spread your money into a lot of different investment types, industries, and companies, you can reduce your risk and hopefully receive higher returns over the long term.

BONDS: A GIFT CARD TO THE FLOWER SHOP

A bond is unique in that it is not ownership in a company, it's actually an "I Owe You" from either the government or a company. Simply put, if you purchase a bond for $100, you are lending your $100 to an entity who will give that money back to you in a specified period of time with a specified interest rate.

I think of this as being most similar to a gift card to a flower shop, because with a gift card you are making a purchase for a defined amount of money with the expectation that you will receive the same value in return. The biggest differentiator with an actual bond is the interest piece—with a bond, you will receive the same amount of money back *plus* interest, depending on the rate of the bond at purchase.

OTHER COMMON INVESTMENT TYPES

INDEX FUND: An index fund is a type of mutual fund that tracks an index. An index is typically used to measure the performance of a defined group of stocks—for example, the S&P 500 Index is used to measure the performance of the top 500 companies in the United States. Therefore an index fund is simply a mutual fund that investors can buy into that mimics a specific index. A few examples beyond the S&P 500 are the Dow Jones Industrial Index or the Russell 2000.

TARGET DATE FUND: A Target Date Fund (TDF) is a mutual fund that is automatically diversified based on the year you plan to retire. A TDF automatically chooses a blend of stocks and bonds for you, and will rebalance the portfolio's risk distribution as you move closer and closer to retirement.

Do You Need a Financial Advisor?

When you don't know how to do something, your initial reaction may be to either google it or defer to an "expert." There is a degree of comfort in turning to someone who seemingly knows what they are doing to validate a decision that you make. It's human nature to seek that validation, especially when it comes to making financial decisions.

Thus, as you begin your journey with investing, it may seem easier to "defer to an expert" and just go to a financial advisor who will not only tell you what to do, but will also invest your money for you. For a fee, of course. Although every financial situation is unique, most people at the beginning of their investment journey don't need a financial advisor. Early on, and truthfully, even for the majority of your working life unless you come into some major cash, your needs are very simple. With some baseline knowledge about the options available to you and a few online searches, you can construct a long-lasting portfolio, create your automatic transfers, and quite literally "set it and forget it."

The reason I tend to ebb away from working with a financial advisor is two-fold. I'll explain.

1. **FEES:** Financial advice comes with a hefty fee, usually in the form of an annual percentage of your assets under management (AUM). Many advisors charge up to 1 percent per year, which at first might not sound like a lot, but as your assets grow over time, this can result in you paying hundreds of thousands of dollars for someone to put your money into a basic mutual fund that you more than likely could have chosen on your own.

2. **YOUR BEST INTEREST:** Financial advisors are paid on commission. This means that although many of them will provide very thoughtful and good advice, not all of them have your best interests at heart. As a result, you could work with someone who points you to expensive funds or convinces you to purchase useless products so they can make their commission.

At the end of the day, no one cares about your money more than you do. So whether you decide to work with a financial advisor or take your investing journey into your own hands, make sure you take the time to learn enough about it to make empowered decisions in your own best interests!

INVESTING CHEAT SHEET

○ **401(k):** Employer-sponsored retirement plan offered by private, for-profit companies.

○ **401(k) Match:** Additional contributions to a 401(k) made by an employer on top of contributions made by the employee. These matches are made on a percentage basis; for example, an employer may match 50% of contributions up to 5% of an employee's salary. Typically, these matches vest over a period of time.

○ **403(b):** Employer-sponsored retirement plan offered by non-profit companies and government entities.

○ **Vesting Schedule:** An incentive program that gives employees benefits when they have fulfilled a certain contractual obligation. It is common for 401(k) match programs to follow a vesting schedule, meaning over the course of a defined period of time, the employee gains full ownership of the matched funds.

○ **IRA:** Individual Retirement Account

○ **Traditional IRA:** A tax-advantaged retirement account that allows the individual to invest pre-tax dollars and then pay taxes on those funds when they are withdrawn at retirement age. With this account, you reap the tax benefit in the year of contribution.

○ **Roth IRA:** A tax-advantaged retirement account that allows the individual to invest post-tax dollars and withdraw those funds tax-free upon retirement age. With this account, you reap the tax benefit at retirement.

○ **Brokerage Account:** A taxable investment account. This is different from a retirement account and offers no tax benefit.

○ **Stock:** Part ownership in a company.

○ **Mutual Fund:** A pool of money that is used to purchase a basket of stocks. This is an investment vehicle that invests in securities such as stocks or bonds. It follows a predetermined investment objective and is professionally managed.

○ **ETF:** Exchange-traded fund. A hybrid between an individual stock and a mutual fund.

○ **Bond:** A security similar to an IOU. It is a loan—issued by either the government or a corporation—with the intention to raise money. When you purchase a bond, you are lending this entity money with the promise of receiving that money back plus interest.

○ **Compound Interest:** Interest that earns interest on itself.

○ **Diversification:** A strategy that mixes a variety of investments with the goal of reducing or spreading risk.

CHAPTER 5 MONEY REVIEW

To build long-term wealth, saving isn't enough: Investing puts your money to work through a concept called compound interest. When you invest, your money can grow over time. When you save, your money stays stagnant and loses purchasing power due to inflation.

Compound interest is the eighth wonder of the world: This is the concept of your money earning money on itself. If you invest your money early and often, you can take full advantage of compound interest. Time is on your side—start investing as soon as you can.

Follow the Investment Prioritization System to optimize your investment accounts: There are three main layers in an IPS. They include your 401(k) (or 403[b]) plus employer match if you are offered one, either a Roth or a Traditional IRA, and a taxable brokerage account.

Focus on retirement accounts first to save money on taxes: Retirement accounts such as a 401(k), 403(b), or IRA are tax-advantaged accounts, meaning they offer a tax benefit. If you focus on contributing the maximum amount to these accounts first, you can reduce your overall tax burden and keep more money in your pocket.

You can optimize your investment strategy with automation: Automate your 401(k) or 403(b) contributions, IRA contributions, and any additional investments. Doing so will help you stick to a consistent investing schedule regardless of the current economic circumstance.

Every investment comes with risk: There is no such thing as a risk-free investment. To reduce your overall risk profile, focus on diversifying your investments amongst various asset classes. This helps spread the risk across investment types, industries, and companies, and it can protect your money if the market ensures a downturn.

Remember the three main types of investments by using the Flower Shop Analogy: Imagine you walk into a flower shop and are inundated with flowers to choose from. There are so many different types—from a single flower, to a bouquet, to a fancy floral arrangement—and each has different combinations of flowers that have different appearances and purposes. The stock market—and the various types of investments you can choose from—is very similar.

You don't always need a financial advisor to invest: Financial advisors can be an excellent tool to add to your financial toolkit, but they are not necessary for everyone. Make sure you understand the fee structure and purpose of an advisor before you agree to work with one!

Chapter Six

Success Is Hidden in Your Routines

Creating habits and routines that I could stick to changed my life. Those habits and routines helped me create a healthy lifestyle when it came to my diet and exercise, they helped me stay organized at work, they helped me keep my home organized and clean, and ultimately they've helped me improve my finances and save hundreds of thousands of dollars.

Habits and routines change lives; creating good ones can accelerate your progress in every area of your life when done right. When it comes to your finances, one of the biggest markers of success is consistency. Everyone can build a budget and everyone can set a goal, but not everyone is consistent.

There is no point in creating a budget or setting goals if you aren't going to check in on them, make adjustments, and optimize them as your life changes (which it will!). Plus, having financial routines is how you create accountability and maintain momentum on your financial journey. That being said, financial routines need to be created with care; they need to fit into your lifestyle in order for you to actually stick to them.

Enter: Your Signature Money Management System, which is your unique process for managing your money. This system follows a specific structure but is designed in a way that you can adapt to *your* life.

It sets the framework for how you manage your money, when you manage your money, and what actions you take on a regular cadence to ensure your money is working for you.

SYSTEMS > GOALS

"You do not rise to the level of your goals. You fall to the level of your systems." This is a lesson I first learned when I read the book *Atomic Habits* by James Clear. Rather than obsessing over an outcome I hoped to achieve, I shifted my focus to the habits and routines that would enable me to reach it. It completely transformed the way I approach my goals—specifically my financial goals and the money management systems I had in place.

Throughout this chapter, you'll learn how to implement various financial routines and create your own system for managing your money. But before you dig into the details, here are a few reasons why focusing on creating a system will take you further than focusing on setting a goal.

SYSTEMS ARE SCALABLE: A system is a repeatable process. It's a small collection of habits or behaviors that you implement to achieve your desired outcome. Once you've created a system that takes you closer to the outcome you seek, you can easily shift, evolve, or adjust the processes involved to help you reach future goals that may be larger or more complex. In short, once you master the basics, it's easy to get to the next level.

SYSTEMS INSTILL CONSISTENCY: As mentioned previously, a system is a repeatable process. Keyword: *repeatable*. If you struggle with sticking to any type of routine—whether it's a morning routine, a workout routine, or a budget—a system is the answer. When you repeat a process consistently, the results take care of themselves.

SYSTEMS ENABLE LASTING CHANGE: Creating a system is playing the long game. Rather than focusing on a result that feels far away, you are focusing on the journey to achieving that result. When something isn't working, you can adjust it right away. When you see progress, you gain momentum and motivation. This enables sustainable results rather than a quick win.

Returning to your finances, think of every step you've taken up until this point as an input to your own money management system. The final step is creating and implementing the routines to stick to it, which I am going to explain shortly.

NEW WAY

OLD WAY

So You Want to Change Your Life?

....

Odds are that at some point in your life, you've wanted to change something that you're doing for the better. For example, let's say you want to lose ten pounds in six months. You set the goal and you follow something like the SMART Method that I outlined on page 53. You're crystal clear on what you want to accomplish and when you want to accomplish it by.

Six months go by and you haven't lost the weight. What's the issue? All you did was set the goal. Anyone can set a goal. But at the end of the day, a goal is simply an outcome you hope to achieve. If you actually want to achieve a result, you need to put a system in place. Your system is the process you implement to actually reach your desired goal.

So if you want to lose ten pounds, you need to do more than just decide to lose weight. You need to create a system—which is the gym routine you establish and the healthy meals you cook. It's the consistent actions that you take every day with the goal in mind.

Ultimately, focusing on creating a system that you can stick to consistently is the most effective way to achieve any goal you set in any area of your life. When it comes to your finances, having financial goals isn't enough. Most people want to save for retirement, own a home, and go on vacation. The people who actually do these things? They have a system in place to make it happen, with each goal serving as direction and motivation.

WHIP YOUR ASSETS INTO SHAPE

Keeping up with the weight-loss analogy, I want to compare creating your money management system to starting a healthier lifestyle. Imagine it's New Year's Eve and you're setting your resolutions for the year ahead. Your top priority is to start living a healthier and more active lifestyle.

In order to do this, you've listed out all of the steps you need to take. A few of them include:

✔ Weekly grocery shopping and meal prep on Sundays
✔ Organizing your gym bag and getting the right equipment to be successful
✔ Creating a weekly and monthly workout plan
✔ Paying attention to daily water intake

What do these have in common? They all require you to change your habits and routines, as well as to start paying closer attention to the specific area of your life that you want to improve.

Now, imagine that instead of losing weight, your top resolution is to start saving money. If I took the same steps and translated them to your finances, here is what you'd need to do:

Weight-loss Habit	Financial Habit
Weekly grocery shopping and meal prep on Sundays	Weekly money review and planning
Organizing your gym bag and getting the right equipment to be successful	Establishing a financial framework and opening the right accounts
Creating a weekly and monthly workout plan	Creating sustainable financial routines that fit into your life and adjusting your budget every week
Paying attention to daily water intake	Becoming a conscious spender and bringing awareness to every purchase by tracking your expenses

Both goals require *consistency* and the implementation of a *system* in order to see results. This combination is the secret sauce for making any long-term, sustainable change to your life.

The formula is simple; the execution is where it becomes difficult. I can sit here and teach you every saving and investing strategy under the sun, but if you don't have a consistent routine in place to actively manage and maintain your money, it will all be for nothing.

Financial Routines

Here are three routines you can incorporate into your life with varying degrees of attention. You can adopt as many of these as you feel necessary; the goal is to find a sustainable practice that works for your life and doesn't feel overwhelming.

WEEKLY MONEY REVIEW

A weekly money review is a ten-minute check-in that you do once a week. It's something that shouldn't take too much time or effort, but it can dramatically improve your financial situation purely by bringing focus to your money on a regular basis. There are three steps:

STEP #1: TRACK YOUR SPENDING

Take five minutes to comb through your spending from the week. You can do this in a spreadsheet or an app. The goal is to categorize your transactions to understand how much money you've spent and what you've spent it on.

STEP #2: SELF-REFLECT

How does your spending make you feel? Did you overspend anywhere? Why? Taking some time to think about your decisions will let you start to notice patterns and where you can ultimately change your behavior over time.

STEP #3: ADJUST

Make any necessary adjustments to your budget based on your spending review and self-reflection. This could be anything from shifting dollars between categories to changing your saving goal for the month based on new information or events in your life. Remember, your life will change constantly and new plans could arise, so having a flexible approach to your budget is important!

PAYDAY ROUTINE

A payday routine is the routine you follow on the days you get paid (duh!). This routine is great if you have a predictable pay schedule; if you work freelance or part-time, I recommend forgoing this routine and focusing on honing your weekly and monthly routines. The purpose of a routine like this is to avoid having money sitting idle in your checking account for long periods. This is a routine that you can automate if you prefer, and it consists of a few key steps:

STEP #1: YOU GET PAID

Your paycheck is deposited directly into your checking account. At this point, you could also have a percentage of your income directly contributed to your 401(k), if your current employer offers one.

STEP #2: PAY YOUR BILLS

Depending on your pay schedule, once you've received your paycheck, you can pay off any outstanding bills or your credit card.

STEP #3: REACH YOUR GOALS

The final step of a payday routine is transferring your money toward your financial goals. It could be making a payment toward debt, contributing to investments, or moving money to a high-yield savings account for a short-term goal. Making consistent movements toward your goals will help maintain motivation and ensure that none of your goals fall to the back burner.

When it comes to creating a payday routine, keep in mind the nuances of your personal situation. For example, you could get paid bi-weekly on every other Friday. With this schedule, you could use your first paycheck of the month to pay off all your bills, then use the second paycheck to put toward your goals. Or, maybe you get paid once per month and you need to divide up your money all at once.

Another option is creating automatic transfers based on the timing of your pay. You could set up your credit card and bills on autopay and create automatic transfers to different accounts based on your different goals. At the end of the day, just make sure you are tracking your transactions by using your preferred method!

MONTHLY MONEY REVIEW

A monthly money review is a deeper version of your weekly money review. It follows the same steps, but it's important to take each step further to do a full review.

STEP #1: UPDATE YOUR NUMBERS

This goes beyond simply tracking your expenses. For a monthly review, you'll want to track your income, expenses, any debt payments, savings transfers, investment contributions, and your net worth. It sounds like a lot, but if you've been keeping up with your expenses on a weekly basis, it shouldn't take too much extra time!

Tracking your debt payments, savings transfers, and investment contributions is critical because it provides you with a pulse-check on your progress toward your goals. With this information, you can make further adjustments to your plan depending on how you're tracking your different goals.

When it comes to tracking your net worth, keeping this updated once per month during your monthly review is enough. If you have investments, your net worth will fluctuate often and updating it too frequently can become distracting. Ideally, if you are consistently saving, investing, and paying off debt, you'll see your net worth grow month after month.

STEP #2: SELF-REFLECT

This is where you can reflect on how you spent and saved during the month. The purpose of this phase is to understand and identify patterns in your financial life that you can ultimately change or improve. A few questions you can ask yourself:

- How does my spending make me feel?
- How do I feel updating my numbers? Good? Bad? Why?
- Have I accomplished any of my goals? Did any goals change?
- What did I do well? Where could I improve?
- How am I holding myself accountable?

Self-reflection is an integral step, and it's one that is often overlooked or skipped. The difference between financially successful people and those who struggle longer than they need to? Self-reflection, behavior identification, and action.

STEP #3: CREATE YOUR PLAN

The final step in a monthly money review is to create your new budget for the next month. You've tracked your numbers from the month before, you've reflected on what did and didn't go well, and now you have an idea of any changes or adjustments you need to make going forward.

Your life is going to change, and it's normal for your finances to change with it. Think about any upcoming travel plans, events, or abnormal expenses that you need to incorporate into your budget and make adjustments as necessary.

Signature Money Management System

Now that you understand the different types of financial routines that will contribute to your success, it's time to figure out how to actually incorporate them into your life in a meaningful way.

This is where you establish your Signature Money Management System. Simply put, this is your own unique way of managing your money. It includes creating a money map, deciding your money flow, and determining your accountability plan.

I'm going to break down each step, and you can use this information to create and adjust your own Signature Money Management System!

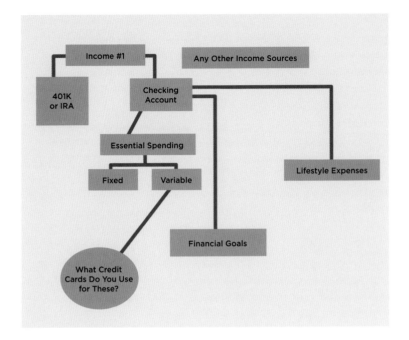

MONEY MAPPING

Creating a money map is one of the best ways to visualize what is currently happening with your finances. Using myself as an example, I am going to walk you through my money map from when I was working a corporate job.

First things first, I had my salary directly deposited into my checking account. I was paid bi-weekly, so on average two times per month. Before my paycheck hit my account, I had 12 percent deducted directly into a Roth 401(k).

From there, my money moved into various accounts. I reserved approximately 50 percent of each post-401(k) paycheck in my checking account to pay my monthly essential bills—such as rent, utility, and insurance. This money is reserved for bills that can't go on my credit card.

Then I used 20 percent of each paycheck to pay off my credit card, which is where I put all of my non-essential spending. I use one credit card for most of my purchases—this helps keep things minimal and organized. Deciding how many credit cards you want to use is an important part of creating your money map. You can have multiple credit cards and give each one a specific purpose, or you can keep everything consolidated on a single card.

Once my bills were paid, I'd make my savings and investment transfers. I reserved 30 percent of my income for my financial goals. The majority of this went directly to investing between a Roth IRA and a brokerage account, and the rest went to short-term savings for various goals, such as my car fund and saving up for travel.

Creating a money map like this can provide a lot of clarity around where your money is actually going. What you want to avoid is having too much money sit in your checking account for long periods of time.

Every time your pay changes, you get a new job, or your bills change (i.e., you move to a new apartment) you should reevaluate your money map.

MONEY FLOW

Your money flow is how you actually make movements between various accounts. This boils down to whether you want to automate everything or manually make transfers on some type of consistent basis that you establish.

To better understand your money flow, you need to identify the cadence of your cash inflows and outflows.

Here is what you need to do.

1. **IDENTIFY YOUR PAYDAY CADENCE:** When do you get paid? Twice per month on fixed days? Bi-weekly every Wednesday or Friday? Once per month? The actual frequency doesn't necessarily matter, but it does determine how you approach paying your bills and moving money around.

2. **DETERMINE WHEN YOUR BILLS ARE DUE:** It's likely you have bills that you need to pay at various points throughout the month. Rent or a mortgage could be due on the first, utilities mid-month, and insurance a week later. It can be hard to manage your money when you have various bills that occur on different days all month long. Make note of when your bills are due on your calendar, along with when you get paid—this will help determine your path forward.

3. **MAKE THE DECISION:** Automatic payments or manual payments? There is no right or wrong answer; it depends on what makes the most sense to you.

If you don't want to spend a lot of time every month moving money around, then you can aim to get all of your bills on the same schedule and set up an auto-payment to pay them all together. You can do the same for your financial goals; determine one day of the month you want to make your transfers, link your accounts, and put them on an automatic schedule. This may take some work up front, but once you get set up, maintenance will be easy.

If you prefer manual payments, you can add reminders on your calendar to pay your bills and move your money toward your goals. You can set a schedule where on the same day of each month you dedicate twenty minutes to moving your money. Ultimately, it comes down to your personal preference as to whether you want to automate everything or do things manually.

ACCOUNTABILITY PLAN

The fortune is in the follow-up, and you need to have an accountability plan in place for auditing your finances and making adjustments as needed. Your accountability plan includes the financial routines you plan to incorporate into your system. Earlier in this chapter, I outlined three financial routines: a weekly review, a payday routine, and a monthly review.

You do not need to do all three of these routines in order to be successful, but you do need to decide which routines will work for your life and how you plan to adopt them.

This could mean selecting the day of the week you plan to check in on your money, putting it on your calendar, and holding yourself accountable to actually doing it.

Personally, I include a variety of all these accountability steps throughout the month, and this keeps me fully in tune with my finances and where I stand. My system includes a weekly money date on Sunday evenings, when I ensure all my expenses are tracked and take a few minutes to update my plan and solidify that I'm on track to reach my goals. I also do a monthly audit, during which I evaluate and self-reflect on where I spent my money and how I plan to change it or adjust going forward. You can build your own Signature Money Management System by creating a money map, assessing your money flow, and implementing your accountability plan. Over time you can optimize your system to fit within the ever-changing flow of your life!

Financial Self-care

When you hear the term *self-care,* you may think of face masks and bubble baths. But self-care is so much more than that; it's all-encompassing and it goes beyond the simple pleasures of treating ourselves to a luxurious bath or skincare routine.

Financial self-care is prioritizing the life you want to live now to align with the life you want to live in the future. It's taking calculated measures to set yourself up financially for the years to come, without sacrificing the things that bring you joy today. It involves connecting your intentions to the way you spend and use your money and finding the balance between treating yourself and planning for the future.

Finding your own financial self-care practice involves developing habits and specific routines around the way you manage your money, as I've discussed throughout this chapter. Ultimately, I want you to think of money management as a positive experience that adds value to your life, rather than causes stress and anxiety around the future.

Here are a few ways to practice financial self-care:

1. **TREAT YOUR WEEKLY MONEY REVIEW AS A DATE.** I always approach my weekly check-ins as more than just a spending review. I will usually go out for a coffee, put some music on, and comb through my spending at my own pace. Because of this, I have made my weekly review a positive experience, and now I look forward to it.

2. **GIVE YOURSELF GRACE.** If you've been implementing new money habits into your life and are still struggling with overspending or if you've been unable to reach your goals, give yourself grace. Often, if you are too hard on yourself when you aren't accomplishing what you set out to do, you can create resentment, which only stagnates your progress further.

3. **SPLURGE WHEN YOU FEEL IT'S NECESSARY.** If you've been sticking to your plan, taking consistent action toward your goals, have implemented a system, and are seeing progress, don't be afraid of the occasional splurge. It's easy to get sucked into doing everything "right," but sometimes treating yourself can bring joy into the process!

As you create your own Signature Money Management System, look for ways to incorporate financial self-care into your new routines. At the end of the day, you're far more likely to stick to a new routine if you actually enjoy it!

CHAPTER 6 MONEY REVIEW

If you want to change any area of your life, you need to change your routines: In the same way that you would implement a workout routine or change your diet if you had a goal to lose weight, you need to change your financial routines if you have a goal to save, invest, or pay off debt. To see consistent change in anything, implementing new habits and creating a system is crucial.

Weekly money reviews will help you stick to your budget: This is a routine you work through once per week. It takes ten minutes and involves tracking your spending, self-reflection, and adjusting your budget. If you have struggled to stick to a budget in the past, this routine will help keep your budget flexible and agile as your plans and spending change throughout the month.

Work through a money audit every month: Reviewing your money at the end and beginning of each month allows you to stay on top of your financial goals. It also will help you uncover blind spots, make adjustments to your budget, and change your spending behavior over time. Take thirty minutes each month to work through this routine and identify what is and isn't working.

Focus on creating a Signature Money Management System and your goals will follow suit: This system includes creating a money map, identifying your money flow, and creating an accountability plan. When you create a system that works for your life, you are far more likely to stick to it long-term and start to see improvement and progress in your finances. In the words of James Clear in *Atomic Habits*, "You don't rise to the level of your goals. You fall to the level of your systems."

Align the life you live now with the life you want to live in the future through financial self-care: Self-care is more than bubble baths and face masks. Make your financial routines feel special by treating your weekly review like a money date, giving yourself grace when you slip up, and splurging when you feel it's necessary (just not all the time!).

CHAPTER 6 ACTION ITEMS

Determine what day of the week you will work through your weekly review: Treat your weekly money review as a meeting with yourself. Put it on your calendar and stick to a consistent day and time every week. Choose this day and add it to your calendar right now!

If you have a predictable pay schedule, create your payday routine: Pull up your paycheck and determine how much you are contributing to a 401(k), how much is deposited into your checking account, and if you want to route any portion of your paycheck into other accounts, such as savings or investment accounts. Remember to take note of your pay schedule and bill schedule, and automate any payments as necessary.

Draw your money map: Grab a pen and paper and map out where your money is currently being routed. Be sure to refer back to the example on page 111 for inspiration on how to do this. Remember to include all of your accounts, credit cards, and goals!

Chapter Seven

Career Conundrum

....

It starts as early as kindergarten: "What do you want to be when you grow up?"

Many kids say "A doctor!" "An astronaut!" "A teacher!" and then, twenty years later, end up working an office job that has nothing to do with what they thought they were going to do.

Some are asked this question so many times growing up that their answer becomes part of their identity; they trick themselves into thinking it's their dream job when really they've just programmed themselves into believing it and end up pursuing a career they don't even like as a result.

Others define success as climbing the corporate ladder. This manifests as getting a huge job offer out of college at a top-tier firm that they've been told all their lives is the best path to success.

And then . . . many people face the same reality; they actually *get* the job they've *thought* was their dream job for their entire lives, only to absolutely hate it, have an identity crisis, and feel like a total failure.

Sound familiar? I've been there. Realizing you hate the reality of the goal you've been working toward your entire life is a pretty tough pill to swallow. The next-hardest pill to swallow? Realizing that your "dream job" isn't real; it doesn't exist, and we've been fed a lie.

I don't know about you, but I do not "dream" of working. I dream of sitting on the beach, sipping a smoothie, and being around family and friends. Work? Never heard of her. Unfortunately, most of us need to work for practical reasons, such as feeding ourselves and paying bills so we have a roof over our heads. And because work is a necessary part of life for many, it can feel like our only option is to be miserable in the path that we determined for ourselves when we were eighteen.

....

Lucky for you, I'm here to debunk this myth. Although many of us need to work, we don't need to be miserable while doing so. We just need to figure out what we like, what we don't like, and the necessary steps we need to take to find a job that fits the bill *most of the time*. Your job isn't, and shouldn't be, your entire life.

Your Dream Job Doesn't Exist

I look back at my five-year stint in corporate America as a learning experience. I learned more in five years of working than I did during my entire life of schooling—college included. Working a 9 to 5 job teaches you about what you want out of your life, how to interact with various types of people, how to advocate for yourself, and much more.

Fresh out of college, everyone goes through a phase where they realize what they've been told about working is a lie. It sucks. All of a sudden your entire life shifts from having complete control over your week, with the exception of a few hours of class, to having zero control over your life between the hours of 9 to 5.

The kicker? Usually the time before or after work is spent *preparing* for work. And so your life starts to revolve around your job unless you step in and change it.

My goal is to intercept you on your career journey early enough that you can avoid living in this reality longer than you need to. With that in mind, here are a few of the biggest lessons I learned while working a corporate job:

THERE IS NO SUCH THING AS "THE PERFECT JOB"

I am about to hit you with the hardest reality check you've been given, so apologies in advance. Everything you've been told about working? It's a lie. Your dream company? It's an illusion. Your dream role? It's not real.

The reality is that most companies, with a few exceptions, are the same. Their highest priority is to maximize their bottom line—it's not to take care of you and give you great experience climbing the ladder. Regardless of what they feed you on their career site, in the interview, or in your onboarding orientation, you need to remember that you are a cog in the wheel of something far bigger than yourself.

This is not a dream. The sooner you separate the emotion from a false vision of your career that you've created in your head, the happier you'll be at work. I know it sounds harsh, but it's the truth—you'll end up better off because of it. Stop searching for the perfect job at the perfect company with perfect benefits. Stop feeding into the glamorized version of office culture that you see on social media. It's not real.

This truth will set you free!

IF YOU HATE YOUR JOB, FIND A NEW ONE

Here's another reality that a lot of people struggle with: You are not required to stay in a job that you hate. I'm not sure why we think this—maybe because conventional school systems condition people into enduring experiences that they don't like, or maybe corporate culture makes people feel like there are time requirements that have to be met before leaving a job.

The truth? Time is fickle. Life is too short to sit in a job that makes you miserable because society told you that you have to or that you'll never be able to find another job because you've only been there for a few months.

In my opinion, everyone gets a mulligan. A mulligan is a do-over or a second chance, and you can apply this to your career if you're really unhappy at work. It may not seem like it, but there are too many jobs out there for you to waste your time in one that is toxic or not giving you what you need.

Not sure if you hate your job or you just haven't been there long enough? Usually, you can gauge if a job is a good fit within the first three months. If you've learned the responsibilities of your role, met the people you will be interacting with the most, have given it a few months, and hate your life every day when you show up for work, it could be time to exercise your mulligan.

You get one mulligan every ten years. Don't become a job hopper, just make sure you aren't wasting your life away being miserable in a job that sucks.

IF YOU HATE WHAT YOU'RE DOING, CHANGE CAREERS

Most people pursue an entire career even though they've figured out early on that they're unhappy with what they're doing. They hold a completely misguided belief that if they pursue something else, they'll lose out on time, status, money, or flexibility.

And this feeling isn't their fault. You are conditioned to make huge life decisions at an early age. You choose your major in college, and then that dictates the jobs you can apply for and the career path you can take. At the time of this decision, you have *no idea* what you are choosing and what the reality of that choice actually means.

So, gaslighting us into thinking that it's not normal to have a career crisis and to realize that you made the wrong choice is one of society's biggest failures. I'm here to tell you this: It is *normal* for your interests and passions to change. It is *normal* to spend a few years working within a specific career path only to reach a point where you actually don't like what the future looks like and you want to make a change. It is *normal* to want to experience different jobs and to lean into newfound passions based on what you've learned and experienced during your working life.

It's *not* normal to decide your entire life when you turn eighteen and have no life or work experience. Yet somehow, this is the society we are confined to. You can change your career path if you want to (and I'll tell you how to navigate this later on in this chapter). The only person stopping you, is you.

SOMETIMES THE MONEY JUST ISN'T WORTH IT

It's easy to chase a big salary and end up in a role, company, or career that isn't serving you. It's easy to overlook glaring red flags during an interview process when the recruiter flashes the salary, benefits, and bonus in the initial phone screening.

It's not easy to show up to a toxic job every day and deal with a micromanager, unreasonable deadlines, and crushing pressure from every angle. Money tends to be the biggest motivator at work, and rightfully so. I don't know about you, but I never showed up for work because it was fun; I showed up because I was getting paid.

However, there is a threshold of income beyond which any additional pay doesn't actually add value to your life. Once you can comfortably afford your essentials, additional income doesn't always improve your quality of life or happiness. So, although money is important and is absolutely the driving factor of going to work, a super-high salary will never be worth your emotional well-being if you hate your job.

YOU ARE NOT DESTINED TO BE MISERABLE

So far, I haven't done a great job of selling all the benefits of working a corporate job. This is because a lot of people are miserable working corporate. They think it's their only option for financial security, and they are so afraid of losing their bi-weekly paycheck that even the idea of exploring a career outside of the confines of corporate feels so far-fetched that it would be nearly impossible.

Misery is not your destiny. You can find happiness in your career, even in the mundane parts of it, and even if you work a corporate job. You can also find happiness forging your own path, outside of corporate America, if that is what you choose. At the end of the day, working does not equal misery, but you have to be willing to make uncomfortable changes in your life in order to find your unique path.

BENEFITS OF WORKING A 9 TO 5 JOB

A 9 to 5 job gets a bad rap, but there are a lot of amazing benefits to working one.

Stability: You have predictable work hours, a set pay schedule, health benefits, and predetermined vacation time and holidays. The work is consistent and your pay is guaranteed, which provides a lot of security, especially when making big life or financial decisions.

Benefits: Corporate jobs offer benefits that are difficult to replace on your own. Health insurance, a 401(k) match, bonus payouts, equity, paid vacation time—these all go away if you decide to start a business and work for yourself.

Work-life balance: With most (but unfortunately, not all) 9 to 5 jobs, there is work-life balance. You know that you'll be working 9 am to 5 pm during the week with weekends off to enjoy your free time. You can close your computer at 5 pm and pivot your focus to other areas of your life.

Social interaction: If you like the people you work with, having a 9 to 5 includes built-in social time. It's a great way to make friends and interact with people during the day, especially if you work in an office that fosters camaraderie.

What Is Your Definition of Success?

Job satisfaction is defined as the level of contentment you feel at work. But what does this mean?

It's a combination of how you feel about your role, daily duties and responsibilities, team members, company culture, company mission, compensation, work–life balance, and more. It goes far beyond what you're doing every single day and permeates all aspects of your experience of actually working for the company.

How do you determine if you're satisfied at work? You need to define your metrics of success. Success is going to look different for everyone, so think about what it looks like for you. For me, initially at least, success was working in finance and having a title that sounded good. It was being promoted, getting a bonus, passing exams, and receiving recognition from leadership and my peers at work. Work–life balance wasn't a priority, nor was company culture; I wanted to feel important and for others to think that what I did was important.

As I've progressed through my career, my definition has changed. Looking back with hindsight knowing that my career journey ended up being so different from what I initially thought it would be, that definition of success is ludicrous to me. In fact, *now* I would look at that definition of success and call it a failure. A failure to myself, my interests, and my life.

I no longer define career success as corporate achievements and climbing the ladder. I no longer put my career and my life into separate silos; they are deeply intertwined, and the balance between them is how I define my own metrics of success. To me, success is my lifestyle. Do I have freedom over my time? Am I empowered to make decisions about my work that have a positive impact on my life? Do I have any passion for the work that I am doing? Is my work impacting the lives of others?

I don't care about job titles or external validation. I don't care if other people respect my career choices or if they even understand what I do. What matters to me is that *I* love what I do and that *I* am happy on a daily basis.

This is how I now define success. With these metrics, I'm able to find *my own* definition of job satisfaction and make the necessary changes as they come up in my life.

How can you define your own metrics of success at work and determine whether you are satisfied with your job and career trajectory? Here are some thought-starters:

1. **WHAT TYPE OF LIFESTYLE DO YOU WANT TO LIVE?** Your lifestyle is a choice; the question is, are you making decisions that allow you to have the lifestyle that you want? Your job has a direct impact on your lifestyle—whether you are working in an office, whether you are working from home, if you are compensated appropriately . . . the list goes on.

2. **WHAT DO YOU WANT TO GET OUT OF YOUR WORK?** This one is very individualized and could change throughout your career. Everyone shows up to work and chooses a job for a reason: It could be the money, the experience, the people, or the work–life balance. Think about what you want to get out of your job. Some people are happy collecting a paycheck and doing a boring job, knowing that at 5 pm they can shut it off and go about their lives. Others are looking for a challenge and want to commit extra time to learning and problem-solving. What do you want?

3. **WHAT DO YOU ENJOY DOING?** One of the reasons so many people are unable to find satisfaction at work is because they have zero passion for or interest in what they are doing on a daily basis. You don't need to love every task you do at work, but you need to have a degree of alignment between your interests and your career or you will never be happy. What does that look like for you, and how can you adjust your work experience to align with it?

These questions might have you pondering every decision you've made. If you're feeling stuck in your job, I'm going to share some tactical tips you can use to figure out if you're on the right path.

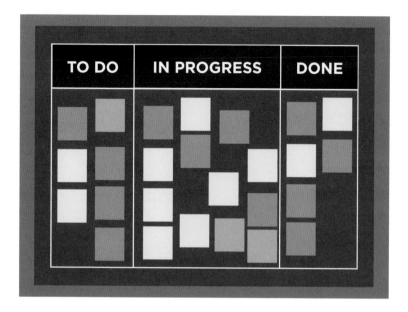

Task-tracking at Work

If you're currently working in a role that you're unsure of, or if you're now questioning whether you're even on the right career path, I've got you. I am a huge advocate of tracking, reflecting, and adjusting; this probably sounds familiar if you've read the prior chapter about financial routines.

Task-tracking and career reflection can uncover many truths that will help you decipher if you're on the right path or not. Here is what you can do.

TRACK YOUR DAILY AND WEEKLY RESPONSIBILITIES AND THE VALUE-ADD FOR EACH

The first step is to start tracking everything that you are doing at work. Every task, no matter how big or small, has an impact on your job satisfaction. The easiest way to audit if you like what you're doing is to write it all down and then go back and review.

It's likely that you do a lot of work that you forget about, that's outside of your job description, or that comes up unexpectedly. Some of this work may be aligned with your interests, and some of it may be dreadful. When you start tracking it, you'll start to see how much time you're spending on all of your various responsibilities, and if the majority of your time at work is being spent on things you enjoy or things you dread.

Beyond simply task-tracking, start tracking the value-add for your responsibilities. How are your daily tasks contributing to your team, your company, and your goals? Are you learning and is your work adding value? If not, then you may find yourself feeling unfulfilled, which is directly correlated to your satisfaction at work.

VALUE-ADDS AT WORK

Everyone wants to get a promotion at work, but how do you determine the value you bring to the table so that you can clearly communicate your skill set? First, you need to get clear on expectations:

Are you meeting expectations? This is the first step in contributing to your team's and company's goals. To do this, it's crucial to work with your manager to ensure that expectations of you are clearly defined, and that you have role-specific goals to work toward. This way, you can define core objectives and specific tasks that you need to complete in order to contribute.

Are you exceeding expectations? Once you've clarified exactly what is expected of you, you can take measured steps to go above and beyond in your role. This means you are adding value beyond what is expected of you in your role and performing at a higher level.

Here are a few examples of how you can add value at work—keep in mind, these are generalized examples, so be sure to adapt them based on your specific role.

EXAMPLES

Increase sales or revenue: Increasing your employer's bottom line is a surefire way to add tangible value. This looks different for each employee depending on their role. If you work in sales or marketing, it would be clearly measured by the dollar impact your work contributes to revenue. But what if you work in IT or an administrative role? It could be ensuring that sales and marketing have the necessary tools or software to perform their job effectively, or that they have the correct customer service training or paperwork to close the deal.

Improve efficiency or save time: Most processes in the workplace can be improved or made more efficient, even if they currently operate perfectly fine. Think about any repetitive or cyclical process or tasks that you do—chances are, you could automate it, refine it, and make it more efficient. Anything can be streamlined to eliminate unnecessary steps.

Become a subject matter expert: Having a specified expertise that is related to your role, team, or industry is invaluable. Your expertise doesn't need to be the main responsibility of your role, but you can become the go-to expert when someone needs help with a certain type of task. A few examples could be related to company-specific software, Excel, social media, website design, copywriting, branding—think about what is applicable to your line of work.

Adding value to your role or company can have a tangible and material impact on your earning potential over time, as well as your job security during economic uncertainty. Focusing on ways to continuously learn, improve, and contribute to your team and company's success correlates directly with your career success as well.

IMPLEMENT MONTHLY CAREER REFLECTIONS

In the same way that you work through a monthly money review for your finances, you should also start doing a monthly career review at work. Reflection is where you can identify patterns of behavior and start to make the necessary changes to improve your life.

This becomes even more powerful if you are consistently tracking your job responsibilities and value-add. You can use that information to think about if you are actually enjoying your job, what could be missing, what you love and want to lean further into, and what you don't enjoy doing.

Over time, you'll start to learn and recognize what is important to you in your career and what isn't, and this will help you make better and more informed decisions throughout your life.

Remember, there is a three-step process to implementing a monthly review: track, self-reflect, and adjust.

IDENTIFY AND EVALUATE YOUR ACCOMPLISHMENTS ON A SET CADENCE

A major factor in career growth is the ability to communicate your accomplishments in the workplace. It's one thing to be a high performer, but it's another to be able to clearly explain what you do and the value you bring to the table. This skill has the potential to open doors and create opportunities that you never would have had access to otherwise.

A great way to start identifying and tracking your accomplishments is related to regular task-tracking. At the end of every week or every month, as you work through self-reflection, identify any workplace accomplishments you've reached. An accomplishment could be a project that wrapped up, a meeting that you led, a new team member that you on-boarded; it doesn't matter how big or small it is.

This information is valuable and can have a positive impact on your career in more ways than one. It can help you advocate for yourself during performance reviews, translate your work experience onto your resume, and communicate your skills and value during an interview process.

Although you're probably already busy at work and the idea of adding all these steps into your current work routine may feel daunting, don't underestimate the impact that these processes can have. It is really easy to fall into a cycle of complacency at work because you're busy or tired, but a lack of awareness resulting from being complacent is how so many people fall into dead-end careers that they hate.

Choose to be different. Your success and your lifestyle is *your choice.* Are you choosing to be successful with what you do?

LEARNING VS. EARNING

When you accept a job, you are exchanging your value, skills, and time for money. As a result, most people equate going to work with collecting a paycheck. But what you're paid isn't the only important factor when it comes to your job.

There are two main pillars of your work experience: what you learn and what you earn. They do not need to be mutually exclusive, but sometimes they are. You will move through different phases of your career during which one is more important than the other, and it's up to you to decide what matters most.

First, here are some definitions:

LEARNING: Learning at the workplace goes beyond your actual job description. It includes your daily responsibilities, your ability to network and receive mentorship, whether you are honing your skills, if you are able to develop new skills, if you're being challenged, and if you're given additional or growing responsibilities.

EARNING: This one is a bit more obvious, but earning in the workplace is related to your compensation. That being said, it goes beyond just your salary. Earning can include equity, a bonus, a 401(k) match, generous health insurance coverage, and tuition assistance.

How can you determine if you're in a season of learning or earning, or if you should accept a job with this in mind? Here are some thought-starters:

- What do I want to learn?
- Will this job provide me with opportunities to learn?
- Does this job provide resources or pay for opportunities to learn?
- What salary do I want to earn?
- Will this job pay me my desired salary?
- Will this job provide me with experience I can use to earn more in the future?

Your answers to these questions can guide your career decisions. If you are not learning or earning in your current job, it's definitely time to find a new opportunity.

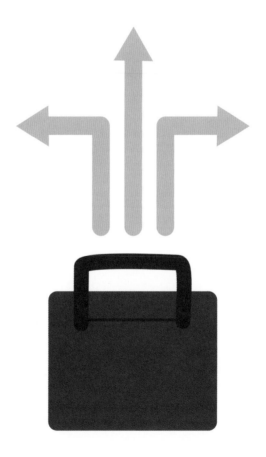

Navigating Career Pivots

Chances are, there will come a time during which you begin to question every decision you've made related to your career. For me, it happened after about three years of working within the investment industry.

For years, I worked for financial companies whose products and services were objectively both boring and unrelated to my life. As a result, I really struggled to actually care about my work, the impact that it had, and the company as a whole. There was no purpose, and this put me on a fast track to burnout.

This is when I started questioning what I actually wanted out of my job. Sure, I wanted to make more money and I wanted to be challenged in my role. But I also wanted to *care*. I realized that to find satisfaction in my career, I needed to be able to find meaning and purpose in what I was doing.

Ultimately, this meant I needed to find a job doing something different—I wasn't going to find meaning or purpose working in the industry that I was in. Making this transition was difficult. I started applying to jobs that were quite different from the role I was in, and it took me nearly six months to finally land an offer that checked all of my boxes.

I've mentioned this already, but realizing that you want something different or that your interests have changed—even after working in a specific industry for years—is normal. You will work for forty-five years of your life, so to think that you'll be doing the same thing for such a long period of time is insane.

If you're feeling the urge to try something new, you can. That being said, navigating a career change can be challenging and requires thoughtful preparation. Obviously, I've got you covered.

Here is a two-phase process for navigating a career pivot.

PHASE 1: DETERMINE WHAT YOU'RE LOOKING FOR

More often than not, switching jobs and changing careers has way more to do with purpose and interest than it does with money. As a result, when you find yourself in a position where you're ready to make a move, it's important to both uncover the reasons why and to think comprehensively about what you're actually looking for. Here is what you need to do:

ASK THE HARD QUESTIONS

Take inventory of what is and is not working in your career at the moment. What types of work are you doing that you enjoy? What are your expectations of your career? What skills do you have that are currently underutilized in your role? What do you want from your manager, team, and company?

Be honest with yourself and think about your values and lifestyle. Your career has a direct correlation with the life you are able to live, keeping both your finances and lifestyle in mind. Do you want to pursue a career path that emphasizes work–life balance? Are you focused on increasing your earning potential and making a lot of money as fast as possible? These are all factors to consider when figuring out what your next move will be.

CREATE YOUR LIST

With the information from your inventory, create a list that details what your ideal job looks like. What do your day-to-day responsibilities include? What type of company do you want to work for? What benefits are you looking for?

With a list like this, you can prioritize different aspects and facets of various types of jobs and industries. Plus, as you begin your search and start interviewing, you can use it as a reference when you evaluate an opportunity and ensure that you are making decisions that are aligned with what you are actually looking for, instead of pursuing a role just because it sounds good on paper or offers a high salary.

LEVERAGE YOUR NETWORK

Your network is your most valuable asset in your career. If you're in the market to make a job switch, start reaching out to connections, former colleagues, and peers who may be working in an industry or at a company that interests you. You can ask questions about their experience and lessons they've learned.

Building your network, nurturing relationships, and leveraging people who you've worked with in the past can have an enormous impact on your job search. The best way to go about this is to make it mutually beneficial; just because you are looking for help from someone else, doesn't mean you don't have anything to offer them! Approach it from the perspective of sharing knowledge and relinquish any expectations or outcomes.

PHASE 2: CHANGE WITH CONFIDENCE

Once you've figured out what you're looking for, it's time to actually get the process started. Making a career pivot is a humbling experience, especially if you have years of work under your belt and are struggling to land an offer. Here are a few tips to keep in mind.

YOU AREN'T STARTING FROM SCRATCH

You already have work experience and a skill set that you bring to the table. The skills you have are an asset, so focus on communicating the unique value and perspective that you have from your prior work history.

FOCUS ON TRANSFERABLE SKILLS

Most skills are transferable from industry to industry. Industry-specific knowledge can be taught, but it takes a lot more time and effort for a company to hone and develop skills. So always emphasize the skills you have and how they apply to the industry or role you are applying for.

KEEP AN OPEN MIND

It's easy to go into a job search with a specific job title or company in mind. A job search rarely turns out exactly how you expect it to, and keeping your options open will make the process a lot smoother. If a job sounds interesting to you, apply for it. If the description asks for more experience than you have, apply for it anyway. You don't know what you don't know!

Finding happiness, satisfaction, and purpose in your career is hard. It's an ongoing journey, and the longer you work, the more and more you'll learn about yourself, what you are looking for, and what will ultimately make you content with your job.

DON'T FORGET YOUR TRANSFERABLE SKILLS!

Transferable skills are essentially corporate currency. No matter what job you work, you are learning transferable skills and can leverage them across roles, companies, and industries if you know how to identify and highlight them. Here are a few examples.

Problem-solving: Every job you work will require a degree of problem-solving. Have you identified inefficiencies or slowdowns at work, and have you proposed or implemented a solution to them? Have you ever been faced with a roadblock or interruption, worked through it, and come out on the other end?

Communication: This one is obvious; at work, you communicate in many different ways, whether it's through email, on phone calls, or in person. What is your communication style, and who do you communicate with? How do you change your communication when you are working with external stakeholders versus internal stakeholders? What do you do to effectively communicate an idea, point, or message?

Analytical abilities: Think about a time that you were given data in any format and you needed to digest it and provide some type of result, presentation, or answer to a question. How have you broken it down into smaller steps? What approach did you take to reach a solution, and were you able to back it up?

Teamwork: Every company is looking for a team player, someone who can collaborate with others and make positive contributions to help everyone succeed. If you've ever been on a team, you know the difference between someone who is simply on the team compared to someone who is part of the team. When have you been part of the team?

Adaptability: Changing due dates, responsibilities, priorities, and even team members is commonplace in corporate America. Can you adapt to an ever-changing workflow and pivot when necessary? How have you done this in the past?

Relationship building: You know the saying: "It's not what you know, it's who you know." Your ability to build and maintain relationships with all types of people and personalities is arguably one of the most important skills you can develop. Think of ways you've built relationships in prior roles and in your life and what steps you have taken to nurture those relationships long term.

Project management: Organization skills and the ability to move a project or task forward is essential in the workplace. Knowing how to manage deadlines, work backwards from an end goal, break it down into tasks or increments to accomplish, and ensure that what needs to happen actually happens is incredibly valuable.

CHAPTER 7 REVIEW

Your dream job doesn't exist: Most people don't dream of working, yet throughout childhood and adolescence, you are taught to pursue a "dream" career. Ultimately, you end up wholly disappointed when you start working and realize it's not all it's cracked up to be. Once you realize that your work is only one facet of your life and does not need to be the driver of your happiness and dreams, you will set yourself free.

If you hate your job, find a new one: You are not bound to your first job or a miserable job. You are in control of your working life. Life is too short to sit in a job that makes you miserable every day.

Take your power back at work: You are conditioned to decide your career path at a very young age. It's normal for your interests and passions to change over time, both as you age and as you gain more working experience. If you don't like the path you are on, you have the power to change career paths. It may take time, but it's worth it.

A 9 to 5 job isn't that bad: There are lots of benefits to working a 9 to 5 job, such as stability, company-provided benefits including insurance and 401(k), work-life balance, and social interaction on a daily basis. Keep these in mind the next time you're having a bad day at work and want to quit.

CHAPTER 7 ACTION ITEMS

Work through a career reflection: What parts of your current role, team, and company do you enjoy? What tasks or projects are you excited about? What aspects of your job do you dislike? What do you hope to accomplish in your career in the next year? What about in the next five years? Are you satisfied with your current salary? Is the trajectory you're currently on going to provide you with the income and resources you need to live the lifestyle you want? The answers to these questions will determine the next step in your career.

Corporate America isn't for everyone, and that's okay: Society's definition of success is going to college and getting a corporate job that you work for the next forty-five years. This path isn't for everyone. If you find yourself struggling in every job you get, don't be afraid to do some inner reflection and explore alternate career paths.

Aim to align your career with your own definition of success: What are your own metrics of success at work? Everyone is seeking something different from their job, whether it is making a lot of money, stability, a predictable schedule, or simply collecting a paycheck and then using your free time to pursue more meaningful work. What are you hoping to get out of your job? Your definition of success will change as you progress through life and your priorities shift.

You are your own best advocate in the workplace: No one cares about your career more than you do. If you want a raise, a promotion, or recognition, you need to ask. You can do this by keeping track of your projects, accomplishments, and value-add on a weekly and monthly basis.

In every job, you should either be learning or earning—ideally both: Learning and earning are not mutually exclusive, but each job you have should be providing you with value. Either you're learning a lot and getting great experience that you can leverage in the future, or you're making a lot of money.

Implement a weekly task-tracking system: In the Resources section, there is a framework you can follow to begin task tracking. Use this as a template to start keeping a log of your accomplishments, positive feedback you receive, projects you complete, and any other information that you can use to advocate for yourself during performance reviews or interviews.

Increase Your Earning Potential

The most basic rule of personal finance is to spend less than you earn. Sounds simple, right? But what if you aren't making enough money to support yourself in the first place? There is a solution: Make more money. A healthy income is a *necessity* for financial success. You can only cut so many expenses, but your earning potential is infinite.

Earning potential, which is the heart of this chapter, is your ability to make money. It is based on the inputs of your career: your employment status, how long you've worked, your employer, your skill set, and more. There are three main avenues you can take to increase your earning potential: asking for a raise or promotion, finding a new job, or starting a side hustle. I'm going to dive deep on each throughout this chapter so you can set yourself up for success no matter what path you choose to take.

I'm a firm believer that your lifetime earning potential is determined relatively early in your career. That is not to say you can't make a career pivot in the future, but the more you make from the beginning, the more potential you have to increase that income exponentially over time.

Looking at my own experience, I spent the first three years of my career earning a salary that wasn't enough for me to excel, both personally and professionally. I knew I was capable of more!

Out of the three options listed above, I chose to find a new job and ask for more money. It worked! Then I added a side hustle, which . . . well, as you can see, ended up working even better. In a short amount of time, the combination of a higher salary and income coming from my side hustle kick-started a new era in my career and ultimately helped increase my earning potential by more than 300 percent in less than twelve months.

That's what this chapter is all about. I'll go through these three options for increasing earning potential in detail.

Asking for a Raise or Promotion

Negotiating a raise or pursuing a promotion is a straightforward way to increase your income and earning potential over time. There are two aspects to focus on when it comes to asking for a raise: preparation and timing.

PREPARATION FOR A PROMOTION

I'm going to focus on preparation first, as preparing for this type of conversation is usually a three- to six-month process. This means that if you want a promotion—which is usually accompanied by a raise—you need to start thinking about it a few months in advance. Here is what you need to do.

KEEP TRACK OF YOUR TASKS

Want to know what makes advocating for yourself, your skill set, and your experience simple? Having proof in hand. You can do this by implementing a few daily and weekly habits into your work schedule.

First, start maintaining a detailed to-do list of your tasks and responsibilities every week. I used to take five minutes to lay out everything I needed to get done on any given week of work. To take this a step further, for each task you complete, try to associate a skill or value-add that the task is contributing.

The benefit of this is twofold: You are ensuring that what you are working on is actually valuable—both to you and relevant stakeholders at your job—and you're actively honing your ability to communicate your experience in a tactical way. To take it even further, you're also fostering a transparent employee and manager relationship and setting the foundation for productive one-on-one meetings going forward.

To-do List	Progress/Due Date	Value-add to Career
Prepare monthly report	Last day of month	Provides insight to management for making decisions
Help on-board new intern	Started—orientation in progress	Learning management and leadership skills
Close deal with new client	End of week	Generate $10k in revenue for new business unit

Next, you need to start keeping track of any unplanned tasks that come up during your workweek. It's likely that you'll get tapped at least once with a task or project that is outside of your regular responsibility. Keeping track of these is essential. Again, the benefits of this are twofold: You are completing work that goes above and beyond your normal responsibility and you are learning and honing transferable skills that add value to your team and company.

Finally, take ten minutes at the end of each week to review everything you've done and highlight two or three accomplishments from the week, no matter how big or small. This is a form of self-evaluation. It's an informal way to reflect on what you're doing, how you're spending your time, and if you're progressing toward your goals. Highlighting weekly accomplishments brings all of the work you're doing into perspective. Many of us do a lot more at work than we think we do, and taking time to reflect on this clarifies value. Plus, by tracking your accomplishments, you can more easily highlight your value in performance conversations when they come up.

GATHER POSITIVE FEEDBACK AS WELL AS EXAMPLES OF HOW YOU'VE ADDRESSED CONSTRUCTIVE FEEDBACK

Each time you receive feedback—whether it's from your manager, a colleague, or a client—jot it down for future reference. You can create a folder on your computer to use as a repository. When it comes time for a performance conversation, you'll have an entire folder of positive feedback from the months prior. This is incredibly valuable, because it serves as proof that you are performing well, meeting your responsibilities, and adding value to the stakeholders and colleagues that you work with.

Beyond positive feedback, keeping track of constructive feedback can also serve as a valuable tool to leverage when you are preparing for a promotion. If you receive less-than-stellar feedback, focus on tracking the ways that you address and apply those learnings and how you plan to approach your work going forward. This serves as a tangible example of how you handle feedback and learn from it.

UNDERSTAND THE RESPONSIBILITIES OF THE ROLE YOU WANT TO BE PROMOTED INTO

This needs to be a major focus of your preparation. Remember, the promotion is just the act; once you get it, you need to actually be able to perform the duties and responsibilities of the role. To ensure that you understand what you are reaching for, take time to map out the responsibilities of the new role as well as how the work you're currently doing can ladder up to the job. How are your current tasks preparing you to succeed and excel at the next level? What gaps do you need to fill? Knowing this information can help you navigate the areas you may need to focus on before you're ready for the promotion.

Implementing these tactics to prepare for a performance conversation may feel daunting, but approach it from the perspective of creating a system for success. Monitoring your progress in the workplace is the best way to advocate for yourself and ultimately increase your earning potential. That being said, preparation is only one part of the equation. You also need to have the conversation—which for most is the scariest part.

BECOME A LIFELONG LEARNER

Take a moment to think about the most successful people you know: They could be well-known entrepreneurs such as Elon Musk or Jeff Bezos, high-performers on your team at work, or people you've met outside your company. What do they all have in common?

Chances are, they are all lifelong learners. They value their education, read about their industry and interests, and go the extra mile to learn, learn, learn. This deep knowledge is valuable on its own but also in what it lets you do once you have it. It will help you think outside of the box. You'll be less afraid to try something new even if it's uncomfortable or the risk of failure is high.

As a result, you'll pioneer a path for yourself that is not only fulfilling, but intellectually challenging and lucrative. And I'm not just talking about successful entrepreneurs! I've come across countless people in my corporate journey who were high performers and forged very successful careers for themselves in the workplace, leading to long-lasting happiness and job satisfaction.

If you're serious about increasing lifetime earnings, then you need to understand the two pillars of making money: earning and earning potential. Most people get caught in the first, looking at earning as the be-all and end-all. This is not ideal because it will make you more likely to focus on short-term gain rather than thinking about your long-term path.

Instead, you need to look at your earning trajectory. This is where you can identify opportunities to increase your earning potential over time. A strong trajectory may not increase your earnings instantly, but it will set up your earning potential to increase exponentially over time.

TIMING IS EVERYTHING: PERFORMANCE CONVERSATIONS

If you're ready to ask for a raise or a promotion, minding the time of the conversation is essential. Most companies offer promotions on a cyclical basis, whether it is bi-annual or once per year. By knowing how this works, you can queue yourself up to align with the cycle and improve your chances of a positive outcome.

Sometimes, a promotion comes up naturally in conversation, especially around performance review season. But, if it hasn't, you'll want to make sure you set up dedicated time with your manager before which you have clearly expressed your intent for the conversation. Here are a few tips for aligning your request with the right timing:

PLANT THE SEED IN ADVANCE

In corporate America, you get what you ask for. If you want to have the conversation, let your manager know a few months before it actually happens. This way, not only do they know your intentions and can take the necessary steps to prepare on their end (such as ensuring there is budget available), but they can also begin to advocate on your behalf and ensure you are getting projects, tasks, and responsibilities you need to prepare for the next level.

UNDERSTAND THE CYCLE

Oftentimes, promotions go beyond your manager's praise or approval. There are bigger factors at play, such as available budget and HR processes. You could be more than ready for a promotion, but if the timing isn't right, you won't get what you're asking for (trust me, I've been there). Knowing the cycle of when promotions usually occur will allow you to set yourself up on the correct timeline and avoid misaligned expectations.

KEEP YOUR MANAGER IN MIND

Your manager is your best advocate when it comes to getting a raise or a promotion. Remember this when you are raising the request and setting up meetings for discussion. If you catch your manager during a busy or inopportune time, you could get overlooked for reasons that have nothing to do with you.

BUT WAIT! WHAT NOT TO DO

At this point, you're well equipped with exactly what you need to do to prepare for your performance conversation and ask for a raise or promotion. You've done the work—from going above and beyond in your role, and highlighting your contributions and skill set, to ensuring that you're on the right cycle—so you don't want to blow it! Here are a few common mistakes people make when they ask for a raise and end up with an unhappy outcome:

YOUR AGENDA IS SELF-SERVING

Saying you want a raise because your cost of living is too high, or you can't afford certain luxuries, is a surefire way to not get what you want. Everyone wants to make more money, but you getting paid more and your reasons for wanting to be paid more aren't necessarily what your employer needs. Most employers want you to be happy and satisfied in your role, but at the end of the day, your employment is transactional. If you aren't bringing additional value to compensate for the raise your employer gives you in return, then you're unlikely to see success.

YOU HAVEN'T PUT YOURSELF IN YOUR MANAGER'S SHOES

What does success look like for your manager and their team? How are you actively contributing to your team's success, and how does that positively impact your manager? Your manager holds the key, and they can either accelerate or block your success. If you don't have their support, it will be really hard to get what you are looking for.

YOU HAVEN'T DONE YOUR RESEARCH

You need to do your research before you have the conversation. This includes understanding the pay range for comparable jobs outside of your organization, but also understanding the pay scale and structure within your organization. Just because your role pays more externally doesn't mean it's a realistic range to ask for internally. Every company has built-in pay scales that have ceilings—you need to know what these are so your expectations are realistic. If you aren't satisfied, you can use that information to find a new job.

YOU OVERPROMISE AND UNDER-DELIVER

Saying that you'll work more hours, take on more projects, and be available at any hour of the day is not a practical way to ask for more money. By doing this, you are essentially begging to burn out in exchange for a higher salary. You want to work smarter, not harder. Think about ways you can optimize your time and efficiency to get to the next level without adding hours to your workweek.

YOU SELL YOURSELF SHORT

This is your chance to convey everything you bring to the table; don't fudge the opportunity because you're uncomfortable talking about your accomplishments or because money makes you uncomfortable. You are at work to get paid—don't forget this!

Changing Jobs

Knowing how to sell yourself, add value in your role, and then communicate that value is tough, but learning how to do this will more than pay for itself. That's because another path to increase your earning potential is to change jobs or career paths.

Changing jobs is challenging. It's time-intensive, it's emotionally exhausting, and the majority of the process is entirely out of your control. But there are strategies you can implement throughout the job-searching process that can help make the experience more positive.

GET CLEAR ON YOUR GOAL(S)

You could be seeking a higher salary, better benefits, more work–life balance, different experiences, or a new career path altogether. Knowing the goal of your search helps alleviate pressure while simultaneously guiding your search to a role that fits what you are looking for.

UPDATE YOUR RESUME

One of the many benefits of tracking your tasks, value-add, feedback, and accomplishments is that it makes it way easier to update your resume because you already have a list of everything you've been working on and achieved. You can use this information to highlight the major accomplishments in your role and create a top-tier resume. Focus on quantifying your value as much as you can—have you helped your company generate revenue, save time, or increase visibility? By how much? This is valuable information to include on your resume because it highlights your skills and abilities while also showcasing how you can help future potential employers.

APPLY, APPLY, APPLY

Apply for as many jobs as possible. If a job sounds even remotely interesting to you, throw your name in the hat. If a job requires more experience than you have, apply for it anyway. The job search is a numbers game, so you increase your odds the more you apply.

A lot of people avoid applying for a job because it asks for more experience or has responsibilities that they may not know how to do, or because they make misguided conclusions about the role, team, or company based on their own assumptions. This is a mistake for a few reasons:

1. **AN APPLICATION IS NON-BINDING.** Just because you apply doesn't mean you're even going to get an interview, let alone get the job, so writing yourself off or assuming that a job is something that it isn't when you haven't even had an initial screening is a self-sabotaging behavior.

2. **JOB DESCRIPTIONS ARE GUIDELINES AND YOU HAVE NO IDEA WHO ELSE YOU'RE UP AGAINST.** Just because a job posting asks for five years of experience doesn't mean that the other applicants fit the bill. You could very well be the most qualified person to apply, even if you don't think you will be.

3. **IF YOU DON'T APPLY, THE ANSWER IS AUTOMATICALLY A NO.** What is the worst thing that can happen when you apply? You don't get a call? Cool, move on.

FOCUS ON YOUR VALUE-ADD IN THE INTERVIEW

You applied to a job and you got an interview—awesome! Now it's time to showcase everything you bring to the table. The recruiter or hiring manager will ask you all the basic questions, from why you are interested in the role to the experience you have.

When it comes to communicating your experience, you want to nail it. How you communicate is *everything*. The benefits of keeping track of your responsibilities and accomplishments on a consistent basis can not only make this process easier, it can also help you become more confident when you communicate your skills.

When you're asked about your experience, you want to highlight projects you've completed, quantifiable value you've contributed, and examples of transferable skills that you can bring to the role you're interviewing for. These could be examples of difficult or challenging situations you've navigated, examples of times you've worked on a team or collaborated with colleagues, or examples of times you've gone above and beyond the regular expectation of your role. You want to answer the question: *What will you contribute in this role, on this team, and to this company?*

NEGOTIATE YOUR SALARY

So you've landed the job and you have an offer in hand, but you're not super thrilled with the compensation package. Many employers will offer a lower salary than they can actually afford to pay under the assumption that you will negotiate. As a result, you should *always* negotiate a job offer (in fact, the best time to negotiate is when you are starting a new job).

Most people don't negotiate because they are either afraid to or don't want to sound rude. I've said it before and I'll say it again: You are at work to be paid. Don't make talking about money weird when it's the reason you're there.

First, you'll want to frame your request around the value you'll bring to the company. This could be through experience from prior roles or through unique skills that you have. If you're able to tie either of these things to the company's strategic goals, you're golden and can likely land on a range that works for both parties.

Another option is to get leverage. The best way to do this is through another job offer. This is why I say you need to apply, apply, apply! The more jobs you apply to, the higher your chance of landing multiple interviews and thus multiple jobs. If you have another offer, you can leverage that to land on the salary you want.

Finally, make sure you enter your negotiation prepared. Ultimately, salary expectations were likely set in the initial stages of the interview process. If you're asking for more, it needs to be within a reasonable range. However, if you learned during the interview process that the responsibilities of the role were different or more involved than you initially thought, you can raise that point and use it to negotiate a higher range.

NAIL YOUR NEGOTIATION

Negotiation is an art; you need to stay calm, be prepared, and remember that it's just a conversation!

You can negotiate for more than just salary:
Consider asking for a bonus, vacation days, flexible work arrangements, or education benefits. At many companies, all of these are on the table during the negotiation process.

Don't be confrontational: If they offer you the job, then they want you to work there! A negotiation isn't about demanding more and walking away if you don't get what you want; it's meant for finding a compromise that works for both parties.

Practice: You're more likely to get what you ask for if you're confident. Confidence comes across in how you speak and what you say. With an offer on the table, the employer doesn't want to lose you, especially after they've put the time and resources into the hiring process. If you practice what you'll say, you'll be far more confident and a positive outcome is more likely.

Side Hustles

The last avenue to increasing your earning potential is a side hustle! Side hustles have become increasingly popular as more and more people have discovered that they can pursue their passions *and* increase their income through starting a business or picking up a part-time job. Let's unpack not only how to figure out the right side hustle for you, but also how to balance it with a corporate job (and ultimately decide whether you're ready to dive in full-time).

FIND YOUR SIDE HUSTLE

There are so many side hustles out there that figuring out the right one for you can be both challenging and intimidating. Here are a few questions to ask yourself as you start your side hustle journey.

WHAT IS YOUR GOAL OF HAVING A SIDE HUSTLE?

Everyone has a different reason for starting a side hustle. It could be to pick up some extra cash every week, or it could be to pursue a passion project, start a business, and quit your job. Getting clear on the end goal of your side hustle will guide how you decide what to do.

If your goal is to pick up some extra cash, it might make more sense to pursue a side hustle that doesn't require a specific skill set or expertise. If the goal is to start a business that you ultimately want to turn into a full-time job, you'll need to approach your side hustle differently.

WHAT ARE YOU UNIQUELY GOOD AT?

If the goal is to start a business, a great way to begin your brainstorming process is by focusing on what you are uniquely good at. When do your friends, family, or colleagues come to you for help? What topics can you talk about for hours on end? What industries would you want to learn about in your free time?

Think about this in the context of your full-time job as well. What skills do you already have that you use on a daily basis at work? Write a list of everything you enjoy at work and see if you can identify some common themes. It's likely you already have a skill or idea that you can use as a starting point.

THINK ABOUT THE TIME COMMITMENT

Regardless of the side hustle you pursue, you need to dedicate specific time to it on a consistent basis to see progress. If your goal is to pick up a part-time job or pursue a low-skill side hustle, you'll want to decide how many hours per week you'll need to work to make the additional income you're looking for. If your goal is to start a business, you'll need to dedicate consistent time on a daily or weekly schedule to get it off the ground. Making extra income requires time, so be realistic with how much time you actually have when deciding your side hustle.

BALANCING A SIDE HUSTLE WITH A 9 TO 5 JOB

If you work full time, the idea of starting a side hustle could feel overwhelming. When I was working a corporate job, I dedicated two to three hours per day outside of my day job to building my business. It didn't take very long for me to become burnt out and overwhelmed. Over time, I learned how to balance both and ensure that I was making progress in my business while also being fully present at work. Here's my advice.

DEDICATE SPECIFIC TIME TO YOUR SIDE HUSTLE EVERY WEEK: In order to make a sustainable income, you can't treat your side hustle like a hobby. A great way to dedicate specific time is to put yourself on a schedule that you can stick to and treat the time you will be working on your side hustle as a non-negotiable meeting or appointment. For example, I dedicated two hours every day to working on my side hustle when I was first beginning. Think about what will work best for your current schedule and be realistic so you don't set yourself up to fail.

BATCH YOUR TASKS: Task batching is one of the most efficient ways to work. Think about all of the different tasks that are related to building your side hustle. In order to get everything done and not get completely overwhelmed, give each day of the week a theme and focus on completing all your tasks on that given day. For my side hustle, I made a schedule like this: On Monday I would film content; on Tuesday I would write copy; on Wednesday I would brainstorm and strategize new ideas … you get the gist!

FOCUS ON THE ONE THING RULE: What is the one thing you can do each day to move the needle forward on your side hustle? When you work full time, there will be days when you don't have a lot of extra time to put toward your side hustle or when you're just too tired to continue working. Think about one thing you can accomplish every day to make a difference, no matter how big or small.

LEAN INTO YOUR PRODUCTIVE TIME: When are you most productive during the day? Are you an early riser or a night owl? Figure out what your most productive time is and build your side hustle schedule around it so you can be as efficient as possible. Remember: Work smarter, not harder!

ACCEPT THE GRIND: A side hustle takes time. In recent years, social media has made it look like starting a business, quitting your job, and earning extra income is easy. This is a lie! If you want to make money, you have to work and accept that in the early stages of figuring out your side hustle and creating your new schedule, you may not have as much free time and you may not make any money right away. Keep going and it will likely pay off.

LOW- OR NO-SKILL SIDE HUSTLES

Are you in need of some additional income but don't have a monetizable skill yet? Here are a few ideas that you can work with.

TaskRabbit®: If you have a toolkit or a car, chances are you can help someone move, assemble furniture, or hang things on their walls.

Grocery or errand services: There are tons of platforms that offer shopping services; you accept a request, run an errand, and deliver the goods for a fee.

Pet services: If you're an animal lover, you can sign up for an app such as Rover or Wag and walk dogs or pet sit. This can even turn into a longer-term gig if you build a relationship with the pet and owner.

The beauty of all these side hustles is that you can create your own hours and work as much or as little as your schedule allows.

CHAPTER 8 REVIEW

If you want a promotion, focus on preparation: Preparing to ask for a promotion is a three- to six-month process. You'll want to gather a list of all your accomplishments, positive feedback, and value-adds so you can advocate for yourself (you can follow the framework discussed in Chapter 7).

Timing is everything: Most companies promote employees on a cyclical basis. Queuing up the conversation a few months in advance and then timing the ask around performance reviews or the cyclical period that your company generally promotes people on will make a huge difference in your success.

Knowing what not to do is just as important as knowing what you should do: Asking for a promotion can't be all about you. Don't make the request self-serving, and frame it up from the perspective of your manager. Your manager will be your best advocate, so make sure you explain how it could positively impact him or her.

Changing jobs is a full-time job: A lot of energy goes into finding, applying for, and interviewing for a new job. To optimize your time, make sure you get clear on why you're looking for a new job (more pay, better benefits, different culture, or responsibility). Then, spend time updating your resume and apply, apply, apply.

Don't be shy about your job applications: An application is non-binding; don't let fear of rejection hold you back from throwing your name into the hat. Even if you don't have all the experience the description is asking for, apply anyway. You never know who you're up against or what the company is actually looking for. The answer is no if you don't try.

When you interview, focus on the value you bring: How you communicate your experience during an interview is what will set you apart from other candidates. Focus on the impact of your work—can you quantify your projects and provide specific examples of transferable skills for the role you're interviewing for?

Negotiate, negotiate, negotiate: The best opportunity to negotiate is when you accept a job offer. Don't be afraid to ask for what you need, and remember that negotiation is a conversation—not an argument.

If you need to make some extra cash, start a side hustle: Your side hustle can be as involved as you want it to be. There are low- to no-skill side hustles, as well as side hustles that require you to learn a new skill and strategize. What are you hoping to get out of a side hustle? Use the answer to that question to guide what you pursue.

Closing Thoughts

You've reached the end of this book and now you're fully equipped with the tools you need for financial success. But how can you be *happy*? Well, that's up to you!

Some say that money buys happiness, and I agree, to an extent. When used correctly, money buys opportunity and experience. When used incorrectly, money creates more problems than it can solve.

I spent years of my life hyper-focused on saving money. I turned down experiences and plans in the name of reaching my goals faster and being what I deemed "financially successful." My family and friends looked at me as the gold star for my age—saving lots of money, being successful at work, and channeling my free time into increasing my income.

But I wasn't *happy*. I thought that the more I saved, the happier I'd become. Sadly, that wasn't true, and it took me far too long to realize it.

Hindsight is 20/20—no pun intended. As the world came to a stop, I had extra time to reflect on the last few years of my life and the changes I wanted to make. It was a dark time for me. I moved home with my parents. I struggled at work. I had virtually no social life. I wasn't able to see friends or enjoy my twenties, and I was feeling a lot of regret.

The saying "you don't know what you've got until it's gone" had never been truer. I had taken my time for granted, and I told myself that once I had more money or reached a certain number in my bank account, I'd be happy and could travel again and live my life.

What I didn't realize at the time was that life can change in an instant, and there really is no better time than the present to do the things you want to do and enjoy your life. If you were to think about the most valuable currency on the planet, most people would think of money. It's not money—it's time. Those are years I will never get back.

Ultimately, I decided to take my life into my own hands and move across the country to California. This was a huge change for me, but one that I knew would be worth it—despite the price.

A few years later, I am living in an entirely different reality. I funded my big move, I say yes to plans, and I have a vibrant social life and a thriving business. I'm not special—but I have made the decision to use my hard-earned money as a tool, and it's created more opportunities than I ever could have imagined. Here are a few of the biggest lessons I've learned.

Live Life Outside the Spreadsheet

You're one decision away from changing your life! This is the biggest lesson I've learned since graduating college. I think it's easy to follow the script: Go to school, get a job, move to an adjacent city or back to the city that you came from, and live the same day over and over and over again even if you're unhappy. Making a change is often much harder.

If you've followed the script and you're not happy, you get to decide to make a change. If you have your financial sh*t together—as you should after reaching this point in the book—then the biggest barrier to making that change—the financing—isn't a barrier anymore. You've equipped yourself with the tools necessary to make smarter, informed financial decisions. Those decisions should enhance your life. If they don't, start making better decisions.

Don't Be Afraid to Spend Money to Make Money

If you had asked any of my friends if I'd ever move to California, they'd have told you there's no chance. I was so caught up in the fact California had high taxes that I never opened my mind to living there until I actually went and saw the lifestyle I could have if I just got over it.

When we're scared to step out of our comfort zones, we make excuses. To me, stepping out of my comfort zone was spending more money than I wanted to. I knew if I moved to California, I'd need to spend more to maintain my lifestyle, and that scared me.

I decided that paying for quality of life was worth it, and it ultimately paid dividends in more ways than one. First, it has opened career doors I never thought were possible. I mean, I'm writing a book right now! If I hadn't moved, who knows if I'd be in this position?

Beyond that, I've traveled, I've made new friends—I basically changed everything about myself in the span of twelve months by changing my mindset and saying "yes" to making plans and booking flights, which also meant I was saying "yes" to spending more and more money on things that mattered to me!

All of these experiences have had a positive and direct impact on my ability to build a business that has snowballed into increasing my income five times over in a very short period of time. If I was still living at home and didn't put myself in a position and environment to take the leap, I can guarantee I'd still be working a 9 to 5.

Say Yes to Life (Thanks to a Financial Plan)

Although I was obsessive over my financial planning, which was admittedly unnecessary, it did enable me to make these big life-altering decisions. Lots of people want to move to a big city or change their circumstance when they're unhappy; not everyone can because money stands in the way.

Financial planning—such as having a budget, emergency savings, and an investing system—puts you in the driver's seat of your life. Money rules everything, and it can either enable or inhibit your ability to experience your life to the fullest.

This isn't rocket science; everybody can do it. Unfortunately, not everyone does because they think they don't have to, or they think that their circumstances will never change. I promise, they will.

What Is Financial Success to You?

Money is a tool; it's a tool that creates opportunity so that you can experience all the world has to offer. For so long, I thought financial success was a number. "When I reach $100k saved, I'll be happy."

Take it from me firsthand, if you aren't using that hard-earned money to live, seeing a number in your bank account will not make you happy.

I asked myself: What was that money doing for me, if it was just sitting in an account, untouched, while I sat at home with no plans and no idea what to do? The answer was nothing. Feed my depression, maybe.

To me, financial success is not letting money decide what I can and cannot do. It's finding work that I don't hate and using the money I make to enrich my life and the lives around me. On paper, financial success is your ability to earn money, to save money, and, most importantly, to spend money in a way that is aligned with how you want to live. But I want you to think bigger: What does financial success mean to you, and how will you use money to live your life to the fullest?

At the end of the day, what is the point of having all this money, if you have no life to enjoy it with?

Resources

WHAT'S NEXT?

Now that you've begun your financial journey, it's time to take your learnings to the next level. Check out the following products and resources on my website www.breakyourbudget.com to dive deeper and get extraordinary results in your finances, career, and side hustle.

DON'T DEPEND ON DADDY PODCAST
Tune in for your weekly dose of tough love and advice on topics related to money, career, business, and routines. Michela answers listener questions, shares personal anecdotes, and breaks down tough financial concepts in an easy-to-implement way.

THE PERSONAL FINANCE DASHBOARD
The Break Your Budget signature financial planning tool. With this comprehensive spreadsheet, you are able to build your zero-based, three-bucket budget; set your SMART saving, investing, and debt payoff goals; monitor your net worth; and more. Inside the spreadsheet you are equipped with all the necessary tools to manage every corner of your financial life, from taking your financial snapshot to working through a monthly money review.

OWN YOUR CAREER TEMPLATE
Ready for that promotion? The Own Your Career Template is the go-to tool for tracking all aspects of your career. Set annual career goals related to your role, performance, and long-term development, as well as track your weekly to-do lists, accomplishments, and more.

BE YOUR OWN BOSS TEMPLATE

If you have a side hustle, you need to manage your business finances and create a bookkeeping system. Revenue, expenses, taxes—it can get very confusing and complicated. The Be Your Own Boss Template helps you organize your business finances, manage your profit and loss, estimate and track your various tax payments, and everything in between.

THE FOUR-WEEK FINANCIAL PLAN

What's the difference between someone who reaches their wildest financial dreams and someone who doesn't? A plan—it's that simple. If you're new on your financial journey and are ready to put together a plan for your money, this course will equip you with the necessary tools to do so. Over the course of four weeks, you are guided through my proven process to create your own annual plan that you can rinse and repeat year after year.

Join the Break Your Budget Community on social media!
Instagram: @breakyourbudget
TikTok: @breakyourbudget
YouTube: www.youtube.com/@breakyourbudget

You can learn more about Michela and review additional resources at www.breakyourbudget.com!

FINANCIAL SNAPSHOT (from Chapter 1)

BANK ACCOUNTS

ACCOUNT TYPE	PURPOSE	REWARD TYPE	AS OF DATE

DEBT ACCOUNTS

ACCOUNT TYPE	PURPOSE	REWARD TYPE	AS OF DATE

INVESTMENT ACCOUNTS

ACCOUNT TYPE	PURPOSE	REWARD TYPE	AS OF DATE

CREDIT CARDS

ACCOUNT TYPE	PURPOSE	REWARD TYPE	AS OF DATE

ASSESS YOUR CASHFLOW (from Chapter 1)

INCOME (Paycheck)		INCOME (Monthly)		INCOME (Annual)	
Gross Pay:		Gross Pay:		Gross Pay:	
Fed Tax:		Fed Tax:		Fed Tax:	
State Tax:		State Tax:		State Tax:	
Medical:		Medical:		Medical:	
Vision:		Vision:		Vision:	
Dental:		Dental:		Dental:	
401(k):		401(k):		401(k):	
Other:		Other:		Other:	
NET Pay:		NET Pay:		NET Pay:	

RECURRING BILLS			
EXPENSE TYPE	MONTHLY AMOUNT	BILL DUE	PAID FROM

NET WORTH (from Chapter 1)

Assets: These are any savings accounts, checking accounts, investment or retirement accounts, etc.

ACCOUNT TYPE	AMOUNT

Liabilities: This is anything you owe, including all debts, such as student loans, credit card debt, etc.

ACCOUNT TYPE	AMOUNT

Total Assets		Total Liabilities		Your Net Worth
	-		=	

SMART FINANCIAL GOALS (from Chapter 3)

SPECIFIC:

What needs to be accomplished to reach the goal?

Who is responsible for it?

What steps do I need to take?

Why do I want to achieve this goal?

MEASURABLE:

How much do you need to save/invest/pay in total?

How will you know when you have reached the goal?

How frequently will you update your progress toward the goal?

ACHIEVABLE:

Is what you are setting out to accomplish realistic?

Do you have the resources or necessary capabilities to achieve it?

RELEVANT:

How does the goal fit into the big picture of your life direction?

Is it relevant to the experiences and lifestyle you hope to live?

TIMELY:

When do you plan to accomplish this goal?

Final SMART Goal:

MONTHLY GOAL AMOUNT

Measurable Amount		**Time in Months**		**Monthly Goal Amount**
	÷		=	

COMPOUND INTEREST TABLE: INVESTING SCENARIO (from Chapter 5)
Investing Scenario Amount: $400 per pay period, $10,400 annually
Time Period: 43 years • Estimate annual return: 7%

YEARS	FUTURE VALUE (7.00%)	TOTAL CONTRIBUTIONS
Year 0	$0.00	$0.00
Year 1	$10,392.00	$10,392.00
Year 2	$21,511.44	$20,784.00
Year 3	$33,409.24	$31,176.00
Year 4	$46,139.89	$41,568.00
Year 5	$59,761.68	$51,960.00
Year 6	$74,337.00	$62,352.00
Year 7	$89,932.59	$72,744.00
Year 8	$106,619.87	$83,126.00
Year 9	$124,475.26	$93,528.00
Year 10	$143,580.53	$103,920.00
Year 11	$164,023.16	$114,312.00
Year 12	$185,896.79	$124,704.00
Year 13	$209,301.56	$125,096.00
Year 14	$234,344.67	$145,488.00
Year 15	$261,140.80	$155,880.00
Year 16	$289,812.65	$166,272.00
Year 17	$320,491.54	$176,664.00
Year 18	$353,317.95	$187,056.00
Year 19	$388,442.20	$197,448.00
Year 20	$426,025.16	$207,840.00
Year 21	$466,238.92	$218,232.00
Year 22	$509,267.64	$228,624.00
Year 23	$555,308.38	$239,016.00
Year 24	$604,571.96	$249,408.00
Year 25	$657,284.00	$259,800.00
Year 26	$713,685.88	$270,192.00
Year 27	$774,035.89	$280,584.00
Year 28	$838,610.40	$290,976.00
Year 29	$907,705.13	$301,368.00
Year 30	$981,636.49	$311,760.00
Year 31	$1,060,743.05	$322,152.00
Year 32	$1,145,387.06	$332,544.00
Year 33	$1,235,956.15	$342,936.00
Year 34	$1,332,865.08	$353,328.00
Year 35	$1,436,557.64	$363,720.00
Year 36	$1,547,508.67	$374,112.00
Year 37	$1,666,226.28	$384,504.00
Year 38	$1,793,254.12	$394,896.00
Year 39	$1,929,173.91	$405,288.00
Year 40	$2,074,608.08	$415,680.00
Year 41	$2,230,222.65	$426,072.00
Year 42	$2,396,730.24	$436,464.00

COMPOUND INTEREST TABLE: SAVING SCENARIO (from Chapter 5)
Saving Scenario Amount: $200 per pay period, $5,200 annually
Time Period: 42 years • Estimate annual return: 0.001% (savings account)

YEARS	FUTURE VALUE (0.001%)	TOTAL CONTRIBUTIONS
Year 0	$0.00	$0.00
Year 1	$5,196.00	$5,196.00
Year 2	$10,392.01	$10,392.00
Year 3	$15,588.02	$15,588.00
Year 4	$20,784.03	$20,784.00
Year 5	$25,980.05	$25,980.00
Year 6	$31,176.08	$31,176.00
Year 7	$36,372.11	$36,372.00
Year 8	$41,568.15	$41,568.00
Year 9	$46,764.19	$46,764.00
Year 10	$51,960.23	$51,960.00
Year 11	$57,156.29	$57,156.00
Year 12	$62,352.34	$62,352.00
Year 13	$67,548.41	$67,548.00
Year 14	$72,744.47	$72,744.00
Year 15	$77,940.55	$77,940.00
Year 16	$83,136.62	$83,126.00
Year 17	$88,332.71	$88,332.00
Year 18	$93,528.79	$93,528.00
Year 19	$98,724.89	$98,724.00
Year 20	$103,920.99	$103,920.00
Year 21	$109,117.09	$109,116.00
Year 22	$114,313.20	$114,312.00
Year 23	$119,509.31	$119,508.00
Year 24	$124,705.43	$124,704.00
Year 25	$129,901.56	$129,900.00
Year 26	$135,097.69	$135,096.00
Year 27	$140,293.82	$140,292.00
Year 28	$145,489.96	$145,488.00
Year 29	$150,686.11	$150,684.00
Year 30	$155,882.26	$155,880.00
Year 31	$161,078.42	$161,076.00
Year 32	$166,274.58	$166,272.00
Year 33	$171,470.74	$171,468.00
Year 34	$176,666.91	$176,664.00
Year 35	$181,863.09	$181,860.00
Year 36	$187,059.27	$187,056.00
Year 37	$192,255.46	$192,252.00
Year 38	$197,451.65	$197,448.00
Year 39	$202,647.85	$202,644.00
Year 40	$207,844.05	$207,840.00
Year 41	$213,040.26	$213,036.00
Year 42	$218,236.47	$218,232.00

BUILD YOUR BUDGET (from Chapter 2)

YOUR INCOME (per paycheck)				
GROSS INCOME	NET INCOME	TAXES	INSURANCE	401(K)

YOUR INCOME (per month)				
GROSS INCOME	NET INCOME	TAXES	INSURANCE	401(K)

ESSENTIAL BILLS			
EXPENSE TYPE	MONTHLY AMOUNT	BILL DUE	PAID FROM

NON-ESSENTIAL BILLS

EXPENSE TYPE	MONTHLY AMOUNT	BILL DUE	PAID FROM

CAREER TASK TRACKING TEMPLATE (from Chapter 7)

PRIORITY	WEEKLY TO-DO LIST	PROGRESS/STATUS	VALUE ADD
1			
2			
3			
4			
5			

PRIORITY	FOLLOW-UPS	PROGRESS/STATUS	STAKEHOLDER
1			
2			
3			
4			
5			

PRIORITY	UNPLANNED ASKS	PROGRESS/STATUS	VALUE ADD
1			
2			
3			
4			
5			

WEEKLY ACCOMPLISHMENTS

Acknowledgments

Writing a book was an achievement I never thought possible. The process has been both challenging and rewarding in ways I never would have expected or imagined. None of this would be possible without my family, my friends, and the wonderful team at Quarto.

First and foremost, I'd like to thank my parents, Lisa and Michael Allocca, for enabling me to carve my own path. You've taught me how to be independent and steadfast in my decisions, and you've provided me with both the space and the opportunity to take leaps of faith that changed my life for the better. Your undying support means the world to me, and I would be nothing without both of you.

To my sister, Alex, who has been a never-ending fountain of advice, tips, and ideas throughout my entire journey of creating Break Your Budget, my writing of this book, and my life. Your support has shaped me into the person I am today.

To my Grandpa, Paul Von Rhee, for always believing in me and cheering me on from the sidelines. Your belief in my success has given me the confidence to make my own way, and I am forever grateful for your support.

Finally, I'd like to thank everyone on the Quarto team for working with me to make this book possible. Special thanks to my editor, Thom O'Hearn, for his patience, assistance, and support throughout the entire process.

Index

About the Author

Michela Allocca created Break Your Budget in 2019 as a side hustle while working a full-time job in the investment industry. Like many young adults in their post-grad years, she struggled to navigate the decision-making that came along with having a full-time salary and a newfound career. Recognizing that she wasn't alone in feeling financially lost and directionless at work, Michela created Break Your Budget as an outlet for learning about personal finance with likeminded young professionals—and she was able to save $100,000 by the time she turned 25. Now, she shares her passion for money with the masses and speaks directly to the growing number of young people who are ready to take their financial power back.

Michela was born and raised in Boston, Massachusetts, and earned her bachelor's degree in finance at Elon University. She spent five years working in various positions within the financial industry before scaling Break Your Budget from a side hustle that earned her some extra cash each month to a multiple-six-figure business with nearly 1 million followers across various social media platforms. She currently resides in Los Angeles, where she operates Break Your Budget full time and enjoys the wonderful lifestyle that Southern California has to offer.